Making
UPHOLSTERED
FURNITURE
in 1/12 Scale

Making
UPHOLSTERED
FURNITURE
in 1/12 Scale

Janet Storey

GUILD OF MASTER CRAFTSMAN PUBLICATIONS

Acknowledgements

GMC Publications would like to thank Christiane Berridge and
Jonathan Phillips for the loan of props used in the styled photographs

First published 2003 by
Guild of Master Craftsman Publications Ltd
166 High Street, Lewes
East Sussex BN7 1XU

Reprinted 2004

ISBN 1 86108 301 7

British Cataloguing in Publication Data
A catalogue record of this book is available from the British Library.

Editor: Gill Parris
Designers: Fineline Studios
Photographs: Anthony Bailey
Diagrams and illustrations: Penny Brown

Typeface: Myriad

Colour reproduction by Universal Graphics Pte Ltd, Singapore
Printed and bound by Sino Publishing House, Hong Kong, China

Contents

Introduction

Traditionally, the framework of upholstered furniture is made using cheaper grades of timber, such as beech or pine. In fact, even underneath the most sumptuous antique upholstery the frame was often crudely constructed and only the exposed areas, like the trim and legs, made in mahogany or other more expensive imported woods. Sometimes even these exposed areas were made of cheaper wood, which was then veneered to look like hardwood.

The furniture featured in this book is also designed for its final effect and, although the construction is very strong when finished, the projects are extremely simple. I make no pretensions to fine carpentry and this is not a book of woodworking techniques, but I have adapted the construction methods so that the furniture is easy to make, even by inexperienced woodworkers.

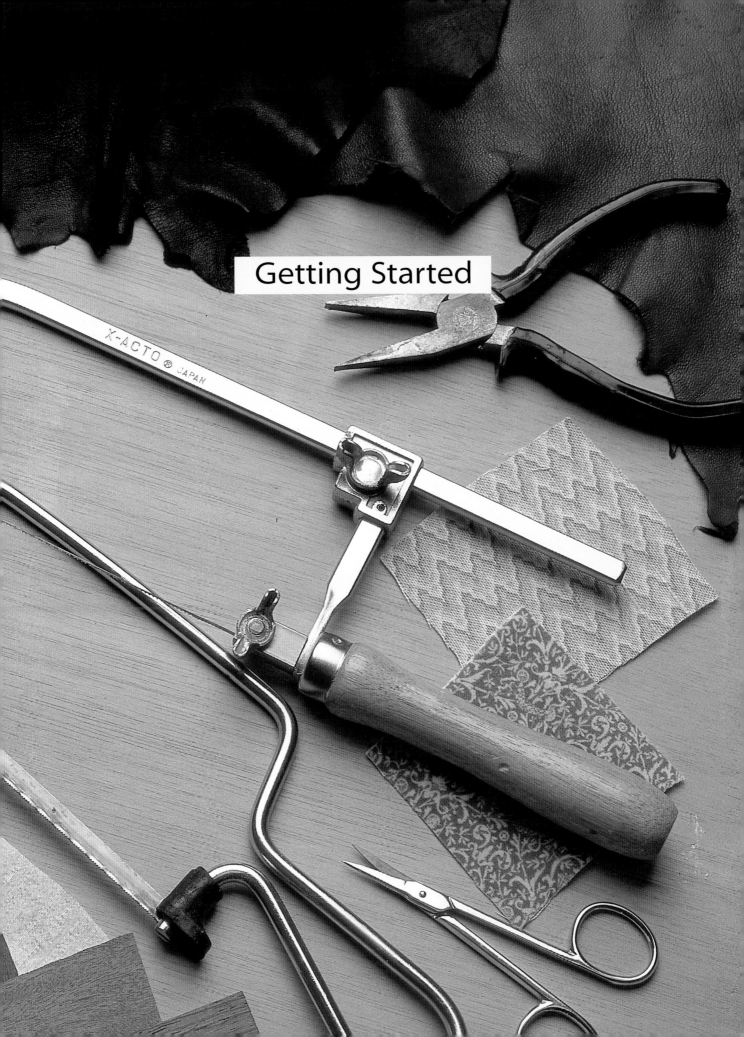

Getting Started

Tools and Materials

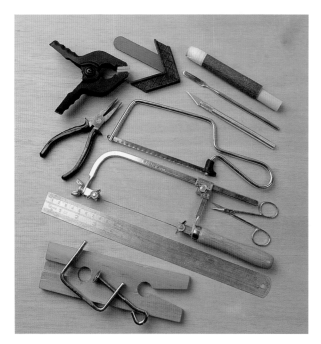

A selection of tools

Tools

- Craft knife, with a very sharp blade. A new blade minimizes the risk of accidental cuts
- Chisel, $1/16$in (1.5mm)
- Fretsaw, either hand or electric
- Junior hacksaw with a flat blade
- Mitre box, for both straight and angled cuts
- Pencil, sharpened to a chisel edge, which is more accurate than a point (rub the point on a piece of sandpaper on two opposing sides)
- Metal ruler, with $1/16$in and millimetre divisions
- Sandpaper, 180 and 240 grit
- Wire wool, 0000 grade
- Woodfinishing materials: wood stain and water-based quick-drying varnish, or French polish and brushing wax
- Wood glue (must be strong and fast-setting, e.g. Liquid Nails)
- Dried silver sand, for filling cushions (see below)

The tools and materials listed are those that I used to make and upholster all of the furniture featured in this book.

The very simple tools are the ones that I use all the time, except when I am making a large batch of one item. Then I use an electric sander and an electric fretsaw, and tape several pieces of wood together and cut them out as one piece, so that all the pieces for that particular part are identical.

Drying silver sand

Spread the sand out on a foil-covered baking sheet and bake in a low oven, gas mark 3 or 100° centigrade, for 30 minutes. After cooling thoroughly, store in an airtight container.

Needles for sewing leather

A needle for sewing leather has a chisel point which cuts the leather, so that the thread passes through without dragging. These needles are available in most good haberdashery departments and craft shops. It is very difficult to pull an ordinary sewing needle through leather, so I would recommend getting one of these, even if it sits in a drawer for a while.

Extras:

- Waxed freezer paper, to prevent glued parts sticking to your work surface
- Large glass-headed pins, for temporarily holding parts together while the glue dries
- Masking tape for the same purpose
- Scissors: small, sharp, pointed scissors that will cut to the end of the blades
- PVA, for gluing leather
- Flat-ended dental tool, or any tool with a flat blunt end (see Suppliers, on page 161)
- Foam sheet, 1/2 in (12mm) and 1/4 in (6mm) thick (available from the suppliers listed on page 161, if you cannot find it elsewhere)
- Needle for sewing leather (see note on facing page)
- Pin-pusher (see right)
- Waxed thread (see right)

Pin-pusher

A pin-pusher is a sprung metal tube set into a handle. The pin is inserted into the metal tube head first, the end of the metal tube is positioned onto the material and the handle pushed firmly forward. The pin will be pushed through the leather and into the wood. It can also be used on bare wood as an alternative to a hammer. The pin-pusher is restricted by the size of the pin it can contain.

Waxed thread

Waxing the thread used for sewing fabric or leather will improve its strength and enable it to pass smoothly through, without dragging or knotting. Small discs of beeswax, which will give the best results, are sold for this purpose in most good haberdashery departments but an ordinary candle can be used at a pinch. Simply pull the thread through the wax, to coat all sides.

A selection of leather

Leather

Leather is sold by the square foot and you will need 2sq. ft (60sq. cm) for each of the projects in this book. When ordering, ask for matched pieces of sheep nappa (sometimes known as gloving leather), as this is thin, stretchy and particularly suitable for miniature upholstery.

I specify matched pieces because they will give you lots of thin edges, which is just what you need for miniature work, whereas whole skins engender too much waste. Pieces are usually cut from the outer perimeter, which is the thinnest section of the skin and, although there may be some blemishes, the upholstery pieces are so small that the blemishes can usually be avoided.

A selection of fabrics. 1, 5 and 10: Silk brocade; 2 and 4: Computer-printed fabric; 3 and 7: Fine velvet; 6: Superfine velvet; 8 and 9: Cotton lawn; 11 and 12: Silk duplon.

A selection of woods. 1: Teak; 2: Jelutong; 3: Oak; 4: Walnut; 5: Yew; 6: Rosewood; 7: Balsa; 8: Mahogany.

Fabrics

To ensure a satisfactory result, choose your fabrics for miniature upholstery with great care. Imaginative use of fabric can hide a multitude of sins, and the appropriate choice can turn a poorly constructed chair into something that you can be proud to show off.

Always use natural fabrics, i.e. cotton, linen, silk or wool, as synthetic fabrics, or polyester/cotton mixes, will not take glue. Even if the bulk of the upholstery is sewn, there will always be times when something needs to be glued and then you will have problems if you use synthetics.

The weight of the fabric is also important. Furnishing weight, i.e. full-size curtain and upholstery fabric, is too thick, so will be difficult to fold and too bulky when more than one layer is required. Also, most upholstery and curtain fabric has a high degree of synthetic fibre in it to improve its wearing capabilities, so it also is difficult to glue.

Conversely, the fine fabrics used for dressing miniature dolls may be just too thin to withstand the manipulation needed in miniature upholstery and it is difficult to get an even finish as it is too fine to hide padding and wood construction. For this reason, I tend to use dress-weight fabrics, as they give enough stability to curve nicely and hide any imperfections in the padding and construction of the chair.

Most suppliers of miniature fabrics will stock some fabrics suitable for use in upholstery, such as fine velvets, brocaded silks and printed cottons, but a rummage in your local dressmaking shop will always turn up a few gems, too.

You will notice that some of the fabrics that I have used for the projects in this book are a bit unusual. This is because I have printed them, using my computer inkjet printer, onto fine white velvet purchased at my local dressmaking shop. I explain how to do this in my first book for GMC Publications, *Creating Decorative Fabrics in 1/12 Scale*. If you do not have access to a computer and printer, a good substitute for these fabrics is miniature stair carpet – the woven-silk type for best results – which is sold in quite long strips at a very reasonable cost.

Sized, unbleached linen, suitable for lining fabric

Stiff fabric for lining

Any closely woven fabric is suitable for lining a furniture piece and for covering the raw edges on the underside of the seat base, but try to choose a fabric which closely resembles very fine hessian or upholstery lining (not curtain lining) in a neutral colour. Thickness is not a problem here and, if the fabric is also stiff, it will help when manipulating into a seat base. The fabric I have used is sized, unbleached linen, as shown above.

Timber

The following woods will make all of the projects included in this book:

- ¼in (6mm) jelutong or balsa sheet
- ⅜in (9mm) balsa dowel
- 10 x 2mm pine strip (only sold in metric)
- 5mm square pine strip (only sold in metric)
- ¹⁄₁₆in (1.5mm) plywood light, or heavy mount board
- ⅜in x ¼in (9 x 6mm) strip wood
- ⅜in (9mm) square hardwood (e.g. jelutong)
- ³⁄₃₂in (2.5mm) hardwood sheet (mahogany, walnut or jelutong)
- ¹⁄₁₆in (1.5mm) hardwood sheet (mahogany, walnut or jelutong)
- Wooden cocktail sticks

I have primarily used jelutong, pine and balsa, because they are easy to work. I have used pine when a particular area needs the extra strength. Any area using jelutong can be substituted for balsa. In fact I recommend that anyone inexperienced with a fretsaw makes the wing shapes in balsa for the first attempt.

Balsa is a much underrated timber, mainly because of its association with children's model-aeroplane kits. Suprisingly it is a hardwood (pine is a softwood) which will get progressively harder as it ages, so don't hesitate to use it for your furniture. Balsa is not suitable for leg construction, however, because the smallness of the legs make the balsa difficult to cut, due to the size of the grain, and the finished legs are prone to breakage. Balsa is not suitable for other areas where the wood shows, either, because it doesn't take wood stain very well.

Methods

Using staircase spindles for legs

The commonly available dolls' house staircase spindle is very adaptable, and the wood is easy to work with just a sharp craft knife.

The type with the square top is the most useful, as the square top can be incorporated into the structure of the chair. This will add strength and stability, and the lower end can be trimmed and adapted for the area of the leg that shows. Alternatively, you can work on just the turned area: cut it to length, dowel, and then either apply directly to the chair, or to a small block that in turn is built into the structure of the chair. Obviously the former method is more stable, as fewer joins in the chair will ensure that it is stronger.

Staircase spindles can vary quite a lot in their thickness, so bear in mind that, generally, shorter legs need to be quite sturdy but, for a taller chair, the legs look better if they are slimmer and more elegant. You can tell immediately if the legs are incorrect for the style of the chair, as the chair will look clumsy and unbalanced.

Gluing: a few things to avoid

■ Never use the glue directly from the bottle, as it will set and block the nozzle, or the water will slowly evaporate from the glue, making it very stiff and eventually hard.

Instead, decant a little glue into a plastic measuring cup or a glue syringe. Don't be tempted to use a pin to stop the glue leaking out of the syringe, or hardening in the nozzle, as the pin will rust very quickly and contaminate the glue. It is better to poke a hole in a small piece of pencil eraser and use this as a stopper.

■ Do not leave PVA on your skin. I have seen people wiping excess glue from their work with their fingers and leaving it on their skin to dry and be peeled off later. Continuous long-term exposure will cause minute amounts of the chemicals to be absorbed into the skin and they will build up in the body, so wipe off excess glue with a damp sponge, or damp cotton bud.

■ Do not leave glue on areas to be stained later, as the glue will form an impenetrable barrier to the stain.

Making the seat cushions

1 Using the chair-seat template for whichever chair you are constructing, trim $^1/_8$ in (3mm) off the sides and $^1/_4$ in (6mm) off the back, then use this as the template for the cushion.

2 Lay the card shape on the back of your chosen leather or fabric and, using a pencil in a contrasting colour, draw around the template.

3 Flip the card shape over and move it $^1/_4$ in (6mm) away from the last drawn shape, but keep it in alignment and draw around it again (Fig 1, right).

Fig 1 Draw around the template twice

4 Allow a $^1/_4$ in (6mm) seam allowance on all sides and cut out the whole shape as one.

5 Fold the leather, right sides together. Sew around three sides, leaving a $^1/_2$ in (12mm) gap at one side. If you are hand sewing, use a small backstitch; if machining, use a medium-length stitch. Use a needle specifically made for sewing leather or fabric at all times (see note on page 4); anything else will cause you much pain.

6 Run a line of glue between the edges of the leather above the stitches. Press the edges together. Do not put any glue across the gap in the stitching, as this gap will be needed for filling the cushion.

7 Trim the three sewn and glued edges to within $^1/_8$ in (3mm), taking care to avoid snipping into any of your stitches.

8 This part is a little tricky to explain, but you need to pinch the centre of the leather on both sides, where the arrow is pointing in the diagram shown below left (Fig 2). Pull the two sides of the leather apart, so that each corner forms a triangle, then flatten the cushion so the seams form a cross on both sides of the cushion.

9 Next, stitch across each corner, as shown in the diagram below right. This will have the effect of boxing the cushion.

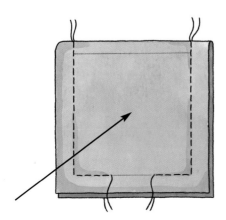

Fig 2 Pinch here (and on the opposite side at the same time)

Fig 3 Sew straight across each corner

10 Turn right sides out (there is no need to trim the corners). Roll the seams between your thumb and forefinger, to help to flatten them.

11 Fill the cushion with dry silver sand (see note on page 4). How much you use will depend on how firm you want the cushion to be, but half full is usually enough.

12 Glue across the opening, to enclose the sand and complete the cushion.

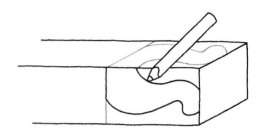

Fig 4 Draw around template on two sides

Cutting cabriole legs

1 Prepare templates marked 'F' on the template sheet.

2 Using wood strip ³/₈in (9mm) square, lay out and draw around on just two sides of the wood (see Fig 4, top right). Do not separate the leg from the wood strip until all of the shaping cuts are made.

3 Place your wood on a fretsaw table or electric fretsaw. Make cut 1 along the line of your drawing, but do not separate this piece of wood at this stage (Fig 5, right).

4 Make cut 2 along the line of your drawing. Do not complete this cut right to the end, leave a little of the drawn line uncut until all the other cuts are made (see Fig 5, right).

5 Flip over the wood, so that the other drawn leg is uppermost and a blank edge is facing you.

6 Make cut 3 all the way to the end of the drawn line, then allow the cut wood piece to fall away (see Fig 6, right).

7 Make cut 4 along the full length of the drawn line as in step 6, above.

8 Flip over the wood and complete cut 2, then cut the leg free of the length of wood. The wood from cuts 1 and 4 should now fall away.

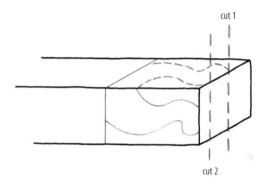

Fig 5 Make cut 1 first and do not complete cut 2

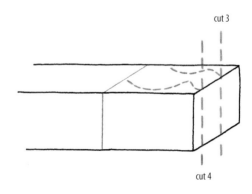

Fig 6 Make cut 3 right to the end and cut 4 to the end of the drawn line

An experienced woodworker may not cut a cabriole leg as I have described, but it does work, so repeat the procedure for the second leg! After cutting, sand off all the edges, including the feet, into a pleasing rounded shape, and finish off with very fine sandpaper.

Finishing exposed woodwork

There are many finishes for wood, including:

- Varnish, with the stain already added: not my preferred method, as I have always had difficulty in achieving a smooth finish with this product.

- French polish: very easy to apply with a brush, but difficult to get a smooth finish on small legs, as early coats dry very fast but subsequent coats require longer and longer to dry. Finally, after about six coats, the polish must be allowed to harden, and by harden I do not mean dry, the polish will be dry very soon after application. The polish needs to go hard before you can consider approaching it with a piece of wire wool and this can take several days.

- Burnishing, which is achieved by rubbing the surface – either after staining, or on the bare wood – with a piece of smooth, slightly rounded wood. This has the effect of crushing the raised grain and can achieve a high degree of shine without any further treatment. This is my own favourite, with the addition of a couple of coats of quick-drying satin varnish.

Finishing legs

1 Coat the whole surface of the legs with a single coat of wood stain in your chosen colour. Allow the stain to dry for at least 12 hours.

2 Take a small piece of wood – any scrap you have available – and smooth and round off one end.

It doesn't need to be perfectly shaped, as the rubbing action when using it for burnishing will improve its performance. In other words, the more it is used the better it works. Use this piece of wood to rub firmly over the surface of the stained legs (or any other piece of wood you wish to finish). The more times the leg is rubbed, the better shine you will get.

3 Next, coat the legs with a single coat of quick-drying satin varnish. Allow the legs to dry for one hour, then coat them again, and allow them to dry for a further hour. Finally, coat the legs for a third time and allow them to dry overnight.

4 Take some ordinary beeswax furniture polish (the solid type, not a spray), or alternatively some finishing wax, and a small piece of 0000 grade wire wool. Apply the wax to the legs sparingly, rubbing the wire wool in a gentle circular movement, within the limitations of the size of the legs. Do not rub too hard, or you will risk breaching the varnish and removing the stain.

5 Take a very soft polishing cloth and rub the legs very hard. If necessary, apply more wax polish. When you have achieved a good shine you should be able to hear the cloth squeak as it is rubbed.

Measuring

Measurements are given in imperial, with approximate metric equivalents in brackets. Before starting a project, decide which set of measurements to use. Metric conversions may have been rounded up or down to the nearest equivalent, so do not mix the two, or you will lose accuracy. I find metric measurements easier to use, as there are no fractions to add up.

Use a metal ruler at all times. To make the divisions easier to see, rub bright-coloured paint into the ruler surface, then wipe off the paint, so that it just remains in the measurement grooves.

11

The Projects

Bolster-back Chair

The first time I saw a bolster-back chair was in a reconstruction of a Victorian bedroom. Two miniature versions of this unusual chair are shown above: the dark red one on the left, with the pink and white trim, is constructed in the same manner as the original full-size chair, while the pink one on the right is made in a very simplified manner.

Materials and Equipment

Thin card for templates

$1/4$ in (6mm) hardwood sheet (not balsa)

$1/16$ in (1.5mm) hardwood sheet or plywood light

$1/4$ x $3/8$ in (6 x 9mm) strip wood

2 prepared spindles or legs of your choice, $5/8$ in (15mm) long

Wooden cocktail sticks for use as dowels

Tacky glue or upholsterer's PVA (extra strong)

A sewing needle and matching thread

$1/4$ in (6mm) foam

Fabric of your choice

Trimmings of your choice

Apart from the obvious differences of trimming and fabric, I would defy anyone to identify the one with the simplified construction. Ironically the simplified version is stronger than the other, simply because there are fewer joints and therefore less potentially weak points. However well a joint is constructed, it will never be as strong as a solid piece of timber, particularly in this scale.

I upholstered the pink chair in silk brocade from a bridal shop, while the red version is upholstered in thin cotton velvet purchased from a miniature drapery supplier. The fringes and tassels on the red velvet chair are hand made and the fringes and tassels on the pink silk version are from cut-down and adapted, bought trimmings.

Here I give instructions for the simplified, pink version. This has a very basic structure, using just two templates for cutting out the body of the chair and one for the legs. The front legs are made from cut-down miniature staircase spindles.

Construction

1 Photocopy or trace the back, seat and rear legs templates below onto thin card and cut them out.

2 Lay the seat template on ¼in (6mm) hardwood sheet and cut out. Sand the sides and very lightly round off the two front corners (see Fig 1, overleaf).

Templates for the wooden framework

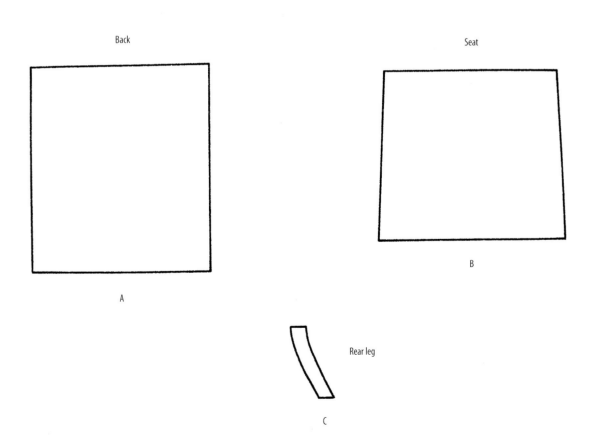

Back

A

Seat

B

Rear leg

C

Fig 1 *Round off the front corners*

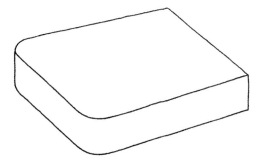

Fig 2 *Taper the bottom edge of the back with sandpaper*

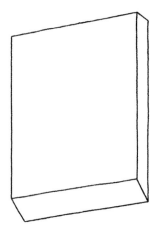

3 Lay the back template 'A' on $^1/_{16}$in (1.5mm) hardwood sheet or plywood light, and cut out. Lightly sand the bottom edge to a slight taper, $^1/_4$in (6mm) up the back (see Fig 2, below left) .

4 Cut two pieces of $^1/_4$ x $^3/_8$in (6 x 9mm) strip wood $^5/_8$in (15mm) long. Lay the leg template 'C' on the side of the wood which is $^3/_8$in (9mm) wide and draw around it. Then lay the template in the same position on the opposite $^3/_8$in (9mm) side of the wood, making sure that the leg shape is curving in the same direction on both sides (see Fig 3, bottom left). Draw around it again. Repeat for the second leg. Cut out the legs with a craft knife or fretsaw. Sand smooth on all sides, and check that the legs match each other.

5 Drill the tops of the legs with a drill bit the same diameter as the cocktail sticks. Snip the tapered end off the cocktail stick and discard it, then dip the cut end into a little wood glue and insert into the hole in the top of the leg. Cut the cocktail stick, leaving at least $^1/_8$in (3mm) protruding from the top of the leg (see Fig 4, below).

Fig 3 *Draw around the leg template on two opposing sides*

Fig 4 *Drill and dowel the tops of the legs*

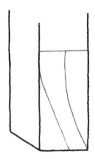

Fig 5 *Mark the position of the legs and drill with the same size bit as the dowels*

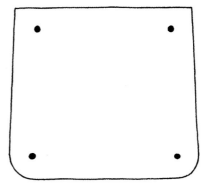

6 On the underside of the seat, mark ¼in (6mm) in from both directions at each corner (see Fig 5, above). Drill a hole at each mark to the depth of the dowel protruding from the top of the legs.

7 Glue the back legs in position.

8 Glue the front legs (the prepared miniature, cut-down spindles) in position.

9 Glue the tapered end on the back part to the back edge of the seat base and tape in position until the glue is dry.

To complete the legs, paint in the colour of your choice. As you can see from the pictures, I painted the legs of both of my examples black, using acrylic paint and several layers of varnish. In retrospect, I think that the pink chair would have looked better with the legs painted in a softer, cream colour.

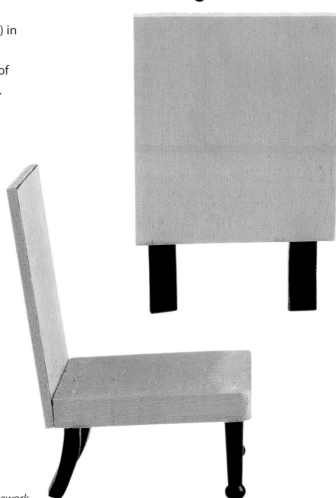

The completed framework

Fig 6 *Glue a strip of fabric around the seat edge*

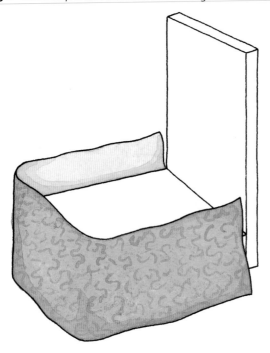

Fig 7 *Glue the overhanging fabric to the top and bottom flat surfaces of the seat base*

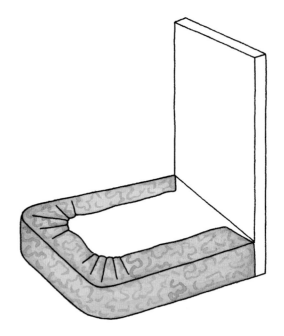

Upholstery

In the period that this chair was first made, fringes and tassels were available in a huge variety of shapes and sizes, so it is not out of scale to use a heavy trimming on a miniature.

Unless you plan to make a second chair, the templates for the seat and the back can also be used as upholstery liners, but you will need to make a second back template.

Do not be tempted to apply silk brocade fabric directly to the wood, as the colour of the wood would subtly alter the colour of the fabric and this would be very noticeable once the upholstery was complete. Instead, either paint the wood white, or glue on a card liner before applying the fabric.

1 Line or paint the seat edges.

2 Line or paint the outside back and edges.

3 Cut a piece of fabric 1in (24mm) wide and long enough to stretch from one side back, around the edges of the seat base to the other side back. Spread glue on the seat front and two side edges. Centralize the fabric over the glue and smooth down. Do not press too hard or the glue might come through the fabric (see Fig 6, above left).

4 Glue the overlapping fabric at the top of the seat, then fold it down onto the seat top (see Fig 7, above right). The fabric will form triangles at the two front corners; pinch these up tight to the seat surface and cut off. Even though the fabric on the seat surface will not be seen, it is best to avoid creating any more bulky layers than necessary.

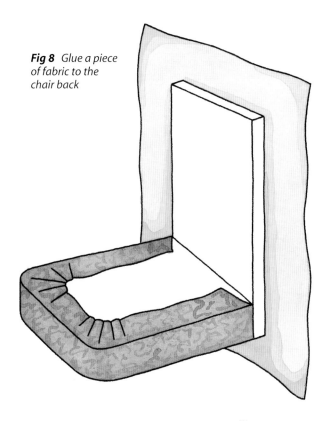

Fig 8 Glue a piece
of fabric to the
chair back

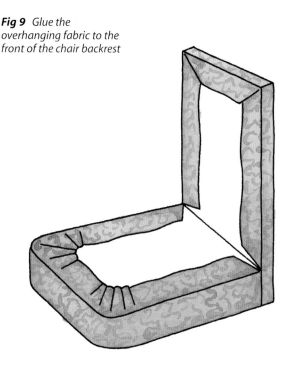

Fig 9 Glue the
overhanging fabric to the
front of the chair backrest

5 On the lower edges of the seat, trim the
overhanging fabric to fit around the legs. Spread
the rear of the fabric with glue and stick down in
the same manner as used for the seat surface.

6 Cut a piece of fabric ¹/₂ in (12mm) larger all around
than the chair back. Centre and glue the fabric
directly to the back (see Fig 8, above).

7 Glue the back of the overhanging fabric on both
sides and the top. Fold over the excess fabric to the
front face of the chair back, pinching the top two
corners in the same way as the chair seat. Snip off
the triangles at the corners (see Fig 9, above right).

8 Check that the chair seat liner is the same size as
the chair seat. Cut a piece of foam to exactly the
same size as the seat liner. Cut a piece of fabric 1in
(24mm) larger on all sides than the seat liner.

9 Lay the fabric right side down on a flat surface,
centre the card liner on the fabric and draw around
it lightly with a soft pencil. Remove the liner and
extend each line outwards ³/₈ in (9mm) (Fig 10, right).

Fig 10 Draw around the card onto the back of the fabric.
Extend the lines ³/₈ in (9mm) at each corner

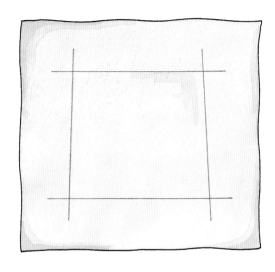

Fig 11 *Sew down the extended lines at each corner*

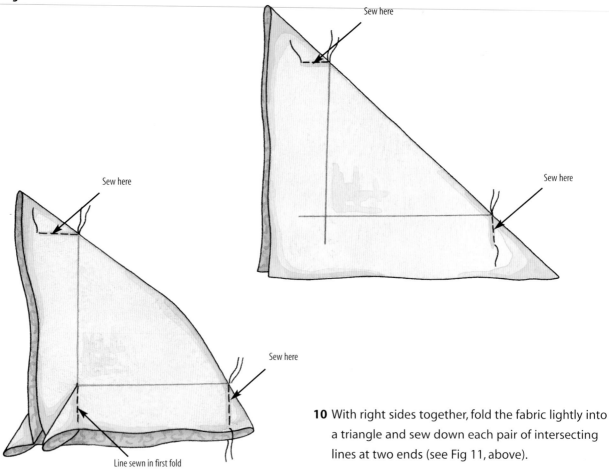

Sew here

Sew here

Sew here

Sew here

Line sewn in first fold

Fig 12 *Re-fold the other way, and sew the corners as before*

10 With right sides together, fold the fabric lightly into a triangle and sew down each pair of intersecting lines at two ends (see Fig 11, above).

11 Re-fold the fabric into the opposite triangle and sew the other two corners (see Fig 12, above left). This will have the effect of boxing the corners of the fabric. If you are using silk do not cut away the excess fabric at the corners.

12 Turn the boxed fabric right side out. Glue the foam to the card and allow to dry for a short time, then insert the card/foam, foam-side down, into the inside of the boxed fabric (see Fig 13, left).

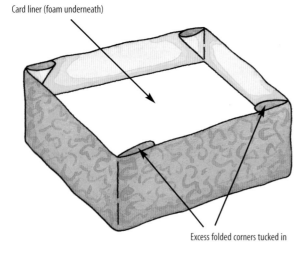

Card liner (foam underneath)

Excess folded corners tucked in

Fig 13 *The card/foam placed inside the boxed fabric*

Fig 14 Fold over excess fabric and glue to the back of the card   *Fig 15* Glue the back of the cushion to the seat base

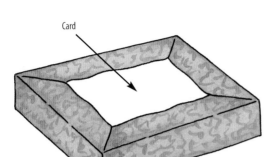

Card

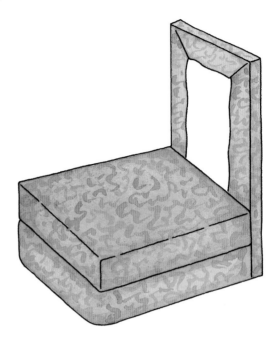

13 To complete the cushion, trim the overhanging fabric to ¹/₄in (6mm) on all four sides, then spread glue on the wrong side of the overhanging fabric and fold over onto the surface of the card, as you did in step 4. Cut off the triangles that form at each corner, as above. Do not pull the fabric too tight or you will spoil the square shape of the cushion (Fig 14, above).

14 Glue the cushion onto the seat base, making sure the glue goes right up to the edges (Fig 15, top right). Do not get glue on the outer face of the fabric, as it is very difficult to remove and will leave a stain.

15 Trim the remaining back liner to fit between the seat cushions and the top edge of the chair back. Make up the back cushion in the same way as the seat cushion. Glue in position.

16 Cut a ¹/₂in (12mm) square piece of foam the same width as the chair back and remove the corners to roughly round it off. Wrap a layer of thin wadding (batting) around the foam and slipstitch the long edges together. Trim the two ends to the same width as the foam underneath. Cut a piece of fabric ¹/₂in (12mm) wider than the foam/wadding roll and long enough to wrap around the roll and

overlap by ¹/₄in (6mm). Centre the foam/wadding roll on the fabric so that there is a ¹/₄in (6mm) overlap at both ends. Wrap the fabric around the roll and overlap the fabric, slipstitch or glue in position (this overlap will not be seen). At both ends sew a row of small running stitches ¹/₈in (3mm) from the end of the fabric, around the circumference (see Fig 16, below).

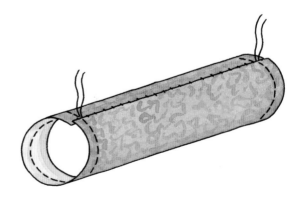

Fig 16 Sew a small running stitch around the end of each roll

Fig 17 *Draw up the gathers at each end*

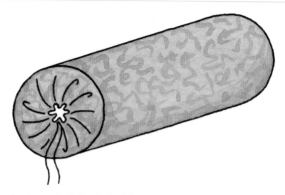

Tie and cut these loose ends off when the glue is dry

17 Draw the gathers up tight and fasten off with
   a few small stitches (Fig 17, above). Repeat at the
   other end, then use an empty ballpoint pen or
   a blunt tool to push the raw fabric at each end
   to the inside of the roll.

18 Dress the chair with fringes and tassels –
   a characteristic of this chair. When applying the
   tassels to the roll, make sure that the fabric join
   remains on the underside of the roll.

19 To complete, glue or sew the roll in position (seam-
   side-down) on the back of the chair (see right).

Small, Buttoned Side Chair

This basic chair, which can be upholstered to fit in any room setting, seems to be timeless. Upholstered in green silk velvet, as shown here, it would fit into any Victorian parlour, although I have been told it wouldn't look out of place in a Victorian bordello, either.

Materials and Equipment

3/8 in (9mm) square balsa strip

3/8 x 1/4 in (9 x 6mm) balsa strip

Small piece of 1/16 in (1.5mm) plywood sheet

3/8 in (9mm) balsa sheet

1/4 in (6mm) square of any hardwood except balsa

2 turned legs, or alternatively, cabriole legs no longer than 3/4 in (18mm)

Fabric (I used a hand-dyed silk velvet)

1/4 in (6mm) foam

Dried silver sand (see page 4)

Trimmings

Sewing needle and thread to match the fabric

Templates for the wooden framework

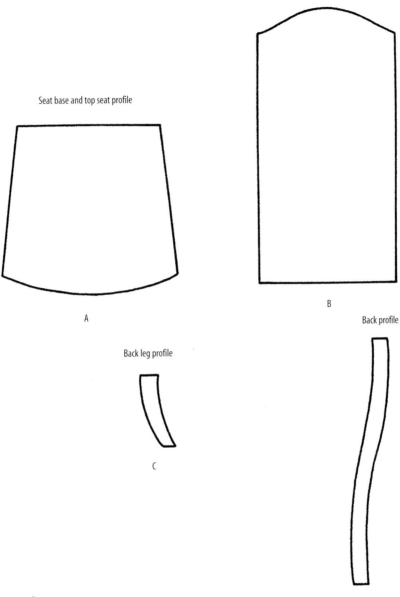

Seat base and top seat profile

A

Back

B

Back leg profile

C

Back profile

D

Construction

Trace the above templates onto thin card, then cut out.

1 Draw around back template 'B' onto ³/₈in (9mm) balsa sheet, and cut the shape out.

2 Place profile template 'D' flat on the side of each long side edge in turn, and draw around, remembering to reverse the template for the opposite side. (You can see the final shape of the back in Fig 3, overleaf.)

3 Using a craft knife, and sandpaper wrapped around a piece of scrap dowel, shape the curves into the back.

4 Draw around the seat base template onto ¹/₁₆in (1.5mm) plywood and cut out.

5 From ³/₈in (9mm) square balsa, cut one piece 1⁷/₈in (45mm) long, for the front of the upper seat base.

Fig 1 *Layout for the upper seat base*

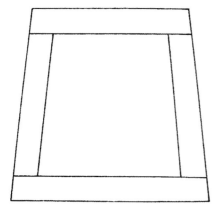

Fig 2 *Lay the seat base template over the seat base and draw around the front profile. Trim away the shaded areas*

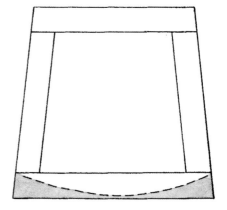

6 From ¹⁄₄ x ³⁄₈ in (6 x 9mm) balsa strip, cut one piece 1³⁄₈ in (35mm) long, for the back of the upper seat base.

7 From ¹⁄₄ x ³⁄₈ in (6 x 9mm) balsa strip, cut two pieces 1¹⁄₈ in (27mm) long, for the sides of the upper set base. Use the upper base layout diagram to get the tiny angles correct (see Fig 1, above).

8 Glue the upper seat base, as shown in Fig 1 (above).

9 Place the upper seat base template on top of the upper seat base, and draw around the front curves (see Fig 2, above right). Turn the seat base over and draw around the template again.

10 Using a craft knife and sandpaper, cut and shape the upper base to the drawn curvature. It is important to ensure that you keep the front and sides vertical during this shaping.

11 Glue on the prepared back, lining up the bottom edge of the back with the bottom edge of the seat base (see Fig 3, right).

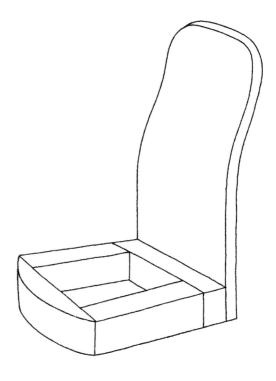

Fig 3 *Glue on the prepared back*

12 Glue on the plywood base. Check all sides to make sure that the plywood is level with the balsa; if not, trim and then sand level.

13 Using the back leg profile template and $^1/_4$in (6mm) jelutong (or other chosen hardwood), cut two pieces $^5/_8$in (15mm) long, then cut and sand the back legs to match the profile.

14 Drill the tops of the legs with a drill bit the same diameter as the cocktail stick dowels. Snip off the tapered end of the cocktail stick and discard, dip the cut end into a little wood glue and insert it into the drilled hole. Snip the dowel to $^1/_4$in (6mm). Repeat with all four legs.

15 On the plywood base, drill a hole $^1/_4$in (6mm) in from each direction at all four corners. The hole must be at least $^1/_4$in (6mm) deep to accept the leg dowels completely. Glue the legs in position.

16 Cut a piece of stiff fabric to fit the surface of the seat. Fill the seat cavity with dry sand and glue on the stiff fabric to contain it.

The completed framework

Templates for upholstery liners, with 'buttoning' positions

Back

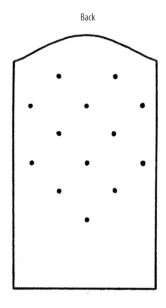

Seat

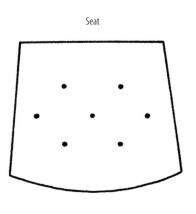

Upholstery

The outer two button positions at each side can be omitted if the template sides need to be trimmed.

1 Trace and cut out the marked templates above. Fit the templates to the chair, with the buttoning pattern on the underside of the card, not facing you. Trim if necessary, then remove them from the chair.

2 Cut a piece of foam the same size as the inner back liner and glue the foam to the <u>unmarked</u> side of the liner, not to the chair. Cut the bottom of the foam to an angle (see Fig 4, right).

3 Cut a piece of fabric 1¹/₂in (36mm) larger all around than the inner back liner. Fold the bottom edge of the fabric to the back of the card liner and glue in position (see Fig 5, top of facing page).

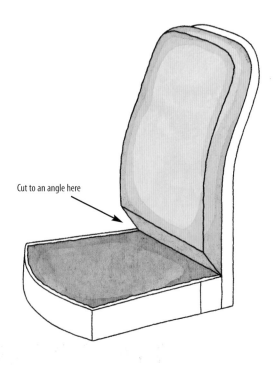

Cut to an angle here

Fig 4 The cutting angle of the back foam

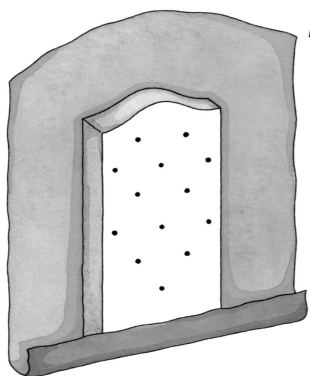

Fig 5 Fold up and glue the bottom edge

4 Take a sewing needle and matching thread and start by pushing the needle through the lowest, single dot, going through the card and out to the front of the fabric. Re-insert the needle $^1/_{16}$in (1.5mm) from the exit point and take it through to the back. Knot the thread but do not cut it free. Continue to the next dot. The thread will form a bridge between each dot. Do not forget to anchor each stitch after working (see Fig 6, right).

5 After completing all the dots, glue the back to the inside back of the chair (see Fig 7, overleaf).

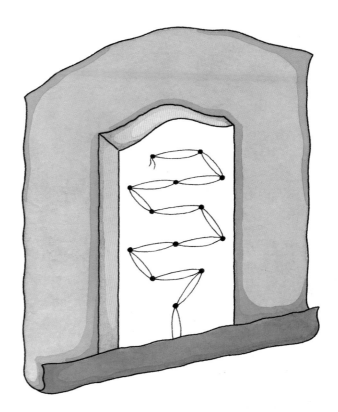

Fig 6 Sew a small stitch at each mark on the reverse of the card

Fig 7 *Glue the card to the back of the chair*

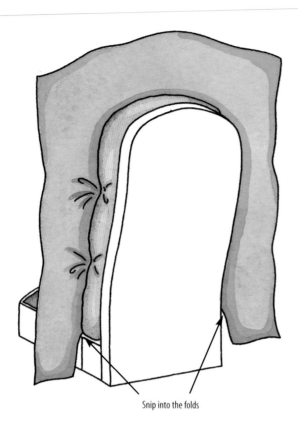

Snip into the folds

6 At the bottom of the back liner where the fabric was folded up initially, snip into the folds so that the fabric hangs down (see Fig 7, left).

7 Glue the excess fabric at each side around to the back of the chair. Spread glue on the reverse of the remaining fabric and bring that to the back of the chair easing in the fullness as you go (see Fig 8).

8 Very carefully remove the triangles that were formed when gluing. This will reduce the thickness when adding the outside back (see Fig 9, below).

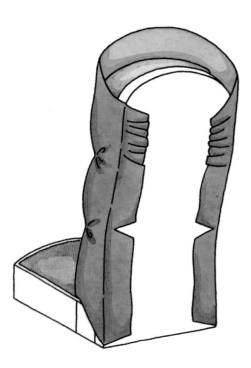

Fig 8 *Glue the fabric at each side to the back of the chair*

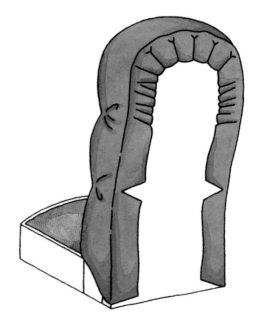

Fig 9 *Gather in the fullness at the top after spreading glue on the reverse of the fabric. Firmly press the fabric onto the back of the chair, then snip off the folds that are created*

9 Fit the seat base liner and trim if necessary. Cut a piece of foam to the same size as the liner and taper the back (see Fig 10, right).

10 Follow the same procedure for the seat covering and application as you did for the back, but glue the fabric to the sides and front curve of the seat base, rather than taking it under the base. Allow the glue to dry, before trimming it level with the edge of the base of the seat (see Fig 11, below right).

11 For the outer back, place card template (B) on the fabric, and cut a piece of fabric ¹/₂in (12mm) larger than the template all around. Glue the template/liner to the reverse of the fabric. Fold the fabric over, and glue to the reverse of the liner at the sides and top, mitring at the top corners. Trim off the excess folded fabric at the bottom corners (see Fig 12, below).

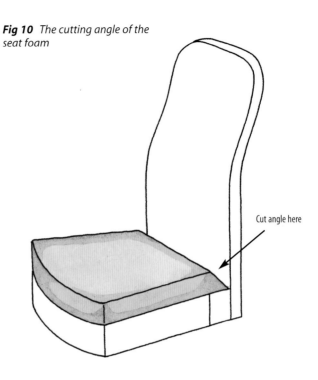

Fig 10 The cutting angle of the seat foam

Cut angle here

Fig 11 Trim the bottom edges level with the set base

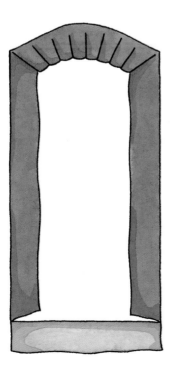

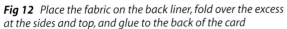

Fig 12 Place the fabric on the back liner, fold over the excess at the sides and top, and glue to the back of the card

Fig 13 *Glue the covered liner to the back of the chair*

12 Spread glue on the reverse of the back liner,
making sure that the glue goes right up to the
edges. Centre the covered liner on the back of the
chair and press in position. Rub the edges with a
flat-bladed tool and trim the excess fabric level
with the base of the back (see Fig 13, right).

13 Trim the seat with fringing,
or braids and tassels.

Chesterfield Sofa

T he Victorians gave the name 'Chesterfield' to this type of large, well-stuffed sofa, which was most commonly found in gentlemen's clubs and private libraries. Traditionally it is a very masculine piece of furniture, and it is only in recent years that it has been found upholstered in lighter, more feminine fabrics and used in general living rooms.

Materials and Equipment

Thin card for templates

$1/4$ in (6mm) balsa or jelutong sheet

$3/8$ in (9mm) balsa dowel

$3/8$ x $1/4$ in (9 x 6mm) jelutong or balsa strip

10 x 2mm pine strip (only sold in metric)

5mm square pine strip (only sold in metric)

$3/8$ x $1/4$ in (9 x 6mm) balsa or jelutong

$1/2$ in (12mm) foam sheet

2 matching leather pieces

Stiff lining fabric (see page 7) and dried silver sand (see page 4)

Needle for sewing leather, and waxed thread (see page 5)

40 Lil or sequin pins, for completing the 'buttoning'

A pin-pusher, optional (see page 5)

Flat-bladed pliers (to pull pins through wood and bend the ends over)

ESP (easy surface preparation paint) for priming the pin tops

Humbrol matt or acrylic paint to match the leather

Ready-turned legs, $1/4$ in (6mm) high (see page 35)/Cocktail sticks

Stain for the legs (see page 11)

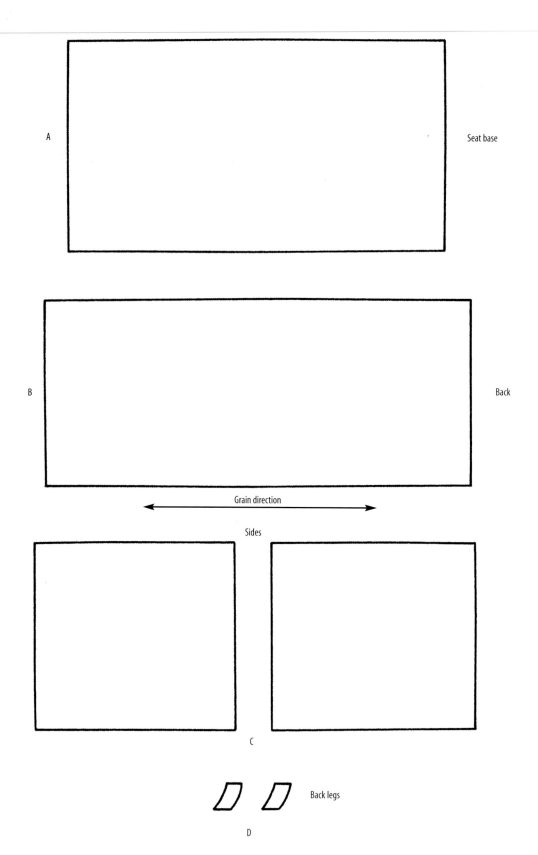

A   Seat base

B   Back

Grain direction

Sides

C

Back legs

D

Templates for the wooden framework

Before you begin

- Prime the tops of 40 pins with ESP then, when dry, paint with matt enamel or acrylic paint to match the colour of your chosen leather (see note, right).
- Photocopy or trace the templates onto thin card, then carefully cut them out.
- Drill $^1/_8$in (3mm) holes in the tops of the legs and prepare dowels: cut off the sharp end of a cocktail stick and glue the blunt end into the drilled hole. Cut the cocktail stick/dowel to $^1/_4$in (6mm) high. Repeat on all four legs, then stain the legs as desired.

Construction

Seat base

1 For the lower base, tape together two strips of 10 x 2mm pine. From this taped wood, cut two pieces for the front and back $4^1/_{16}$in (104mm) long, and two pieces for the sides $1^3/_8$in (35mm) long.

2 For the upper base, tape together two strips of balsa or jelutong $^3/_8$ x $^1/_4$in (9 x 6mm). From this, cut two pieces $4^1/_{16}$in (104mm) long, for the front and back (NB they must be the same lengths as those cut in step 1) and two side pieces $1^{11}/_{16}$in (43mm) long.

3 Lay the cut pieces out on waxed paper and glue as shown in Figs 1 and 2 below. Allow the glue to dry completely before handling, as the pieces are very unstable until the next layer goes on.

Fig 1 *Lower seat base*

Fig 2 *Upper seat base*

Fig 3 *The upper and lower seat bases glued together*

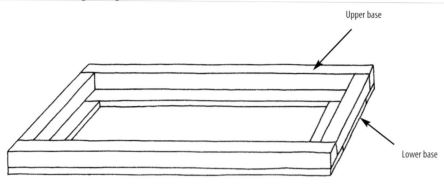

Upper base

Lower base

4 Glue the upper base on top of the lower base, as shown in Fig 3 above, then leave the base to dry overnight, if possible with a weight, such as a book, on top. Do not move the base until the glue is completely hard, or it may slide out of alignment.

5 Once the seat base is dry, check that the sides are level and if not, use a sanding block – i.e. a block of wood with sandpaper wrapped around it – to level the surface. Be careful when doing this as, if you have used balsa for the upper part of the seat, it will sand away faster than the pine beneath it, giving an unwanted slope to the sides.

Back and sides

1 Place the back and side templates (B and C) on $^1/_4$in (6mm) balsa sheet, with the longest sides laid in the direction of the grain. Draw around the templates, then cut out the pieces with a hand or electric fretsaw.

2 Cut a length of $^3/_8$in (9mm) balsa dowel the exact width of the back part (B).

3 Cut two lengths of balsa dowel the width of the two sides (C) plus $^1/_2$in (12mm). Do not to rotate the sides, as the grain of the wood must remain horizontal.

4 Flatten one side of each piece of dowel, each one to the same extent (see Fig 4 below).

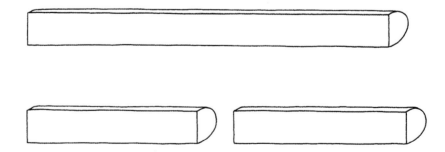

Fig 4 *The dowel pieces with flattened sides*

Fig 5 *The sides and back in position*

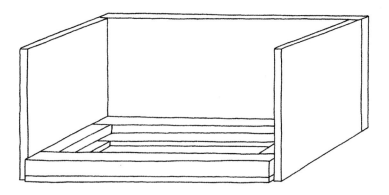

Adding the back and sides to the seat

1 Lay the seat assembly on a flat surface and glue the two sides to the seat so that their back edges are level with the back edges of the seat base.

2 Glue the front sides and lower front edge of back piece 'B', and along the back ends of the side pieces where they will abut the back piece, then fix the back piece in place (see Fig 5, above). Leave to dry.

3 Use the sanding block again to level the surfaces where the back joins the sides.

Adding the roll edges

1 Glue the flattened edge of the longest piece of balsa dowel along the top edge of the back piece, aligning it with edges of the back at each end (Fig 6).

2 Glue the flattened edge of one of the shorter pieces of balsa dowel along the top outer edge of one of the side pieces, making sure all the pieces align. Repeat the process on the other side piece (Fig 6).

3 Use the sandblock to round over the back corners, of the balsa dowel, where the side dowels meet the back dowel.

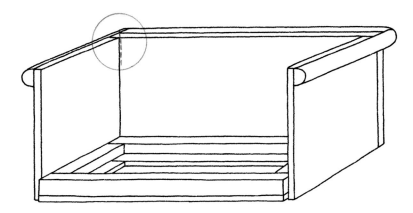

Fig 6 *A detail of the corner is shown overleaf (Fig 7)*

Fig 7 *Shaping the back and sides*

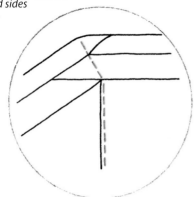

Adding the legs

1 Drill a hole the same size as the cocktail stick dowels in each corner of the sofa base.

2 Glue the legs in position.

3 Finish the legs with your chosen wood finish.

Shaping the back and sides

1 Draw a diagonal line on the back inside corners from the point where the sides meet the back to the outside corner (see Fig 7, above).

2 Run a craft knife into the drawn line and across the top corners.

3 Roughly shape the side and back edges to a gentle curve, using a craft knife, then smooth off with sandpaper.

The completed framework

Upholstery

Before you begin the upholstery, cut a piece of stiff fabric to line the inside of the seat well, then cut a second piece of the same fabric large enough to cover the entire seat area, less ⅛in (3mm) of fabric at the front.

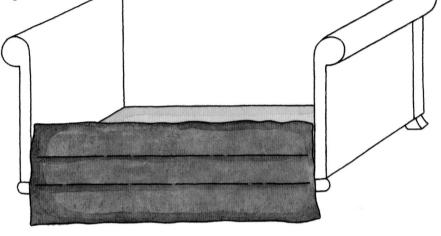

Glue in the seat well covering and, after it has dried, coat the whole area with PVA glue, to prevent the sand from penetrating the fabric.

Glue the piece for the seat cover along the back edge only, and fix it in place. This will form the cavity into which the sand will eventually go to give the sofa weight, but do not fill at this time.

1 Cut a piece of leather long enough to fit the front seat rail exactly, and wider than the rail by ½in (12mm) at the top and bottom. Glue the leather to the front of the rail, then fold over the top ½in (12mm) and glue in position (see Fig 8, above).

2 Fill the seat cavity with dry silver sand and glue down the seat-well covering at the sides and front.

3 Trim the bottom ½in (12mm) overhang to fit around the front legs. Glue the leather in position.

4 Cut two pieces of leather long enough to cover the side fronts with a ½in (12mm) overhang all around. Notch the leather on the curves and under the arm roll. Glue the excess down, as shown in Fig 9, below.

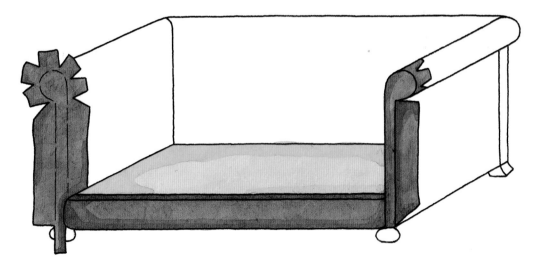

Fig 9 *Adding the leather to the side fronts*

Templates for back and side upholstery liners, showing 'buttoning'

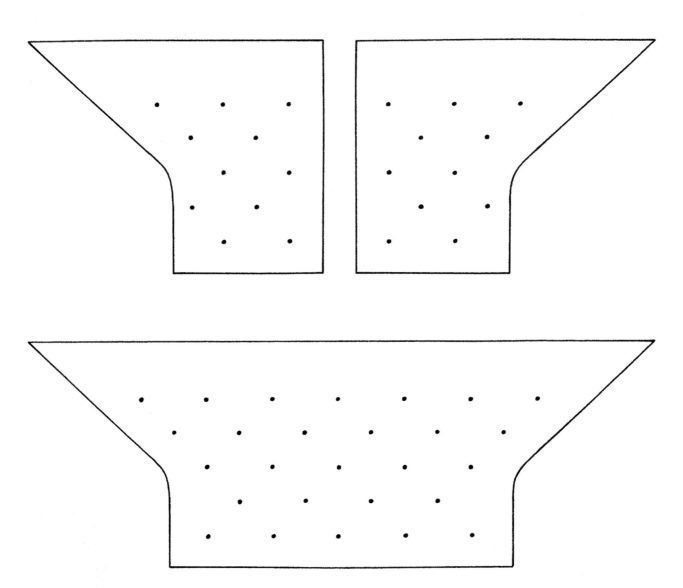

It is very important to transfer all the markings when copying the templates

Note

For correct size this template should be enlarged
by 111%

5 Check the leather at the front rail and side fronts for excess glue. Any excess must be removed before it hardens, or it will dry as a white patch on the leather. Use a damp sponge to remove the glue, but squeeze as much moisture as possible out of the sponge before using, or it will also discolour the leather.

Upholstery liners

To keep the softness of the leather, you should prepare the upholstery liners as described below:

Photocopy or trace the liner shapes on the facing page onto thin card, taking care to transfer all the 'buttoning' markings, then cut out the shapes. Make a second set without the markings and set this one aside until step 5.

1 First, pin the back (marked) liner, to the inside back at the bottom edge, making sure that the markings are on the underside of the card, i.e. next to the wood.

2 Repeat the step above with each side liner, placing the straight edge to the front of the inside arm and the pointed bit to the back, so that the pointed bits of the side and back liners overlap at the corners.

3 Curve the card liner over the back roll and pin in place. Repeat on both sides. The card should overlap the curved area on the back corners.

4 Using small paper-cutting scissors, cut down the centre of both pieces of card at the overlapping corners on each side (see Fig 10, below).

5 Draw around the second set of templates, which were set aside earlier, onto 1/2in (12mm) foam, adding 2in (48mm) of extra foam at the top (widest) edge on all pieces.

6 Glue the foam to the card shapes pinned to the sofa frame, removing and replacing the pins as you go. Do not stretch the foam over the back and side rolls, but allow it to curve gently, while held in position by the pins. If you stretch the foam it will flatten it, and the rolls will not button effectively.

7 Push the sides firmly into the corners. You will find that, because of the added bulk of the foam, the sides will stick out at the front. This is correct and will be sorted out in a later step. Set aside and allow the glue to dry. Once dry, you will find that the card/foam will retain the shape of the back and side curves, which is very important for the final buttoning and for the even thickness of the padding.

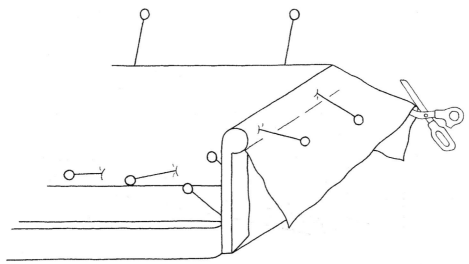

Fig 10 *Trimming the card*

8 When the glue is dry, leave the liners in position while the card and foam are trimmed. The card and foam must be trimmed separately, beginning with the card on the overhang on the arm and back rolls. Hold back the foam and cut the card to the edge of the arm roll – the card must not protrude past the arm roll. Try not to cut off any markings although, if your shaping has been greater than my own, you may find you have to dispense with the top row.

9 Next, cut back the foam until it fits comfortably under the arm rolls without any stretch or strain. Do not trim the overhang at the side front edges at this stage.

10 Remove the liners from the sofa.

Adding the leather

1 Now cut three pieces, which must be larger all around than the card/foam liners, from the thinnest part of the leather. When measuring, be generous and curve the leather over the full extent of the liner and allow at least 1in (24mm) extra at the bottom edge, 1½in (36mm) at each side and 2in (48mm) at the top. The additional leather is necessary, since it will pull in when you do the 'buttoning' for the chair.

2 Glue the leather to the card along the back bottom edge, taking care that you do not cover up any of the markings on the card.

3 Repeat the above process with each side liner (see Fig 11, below).

Fig 11 The leather glued to the bottom of the card

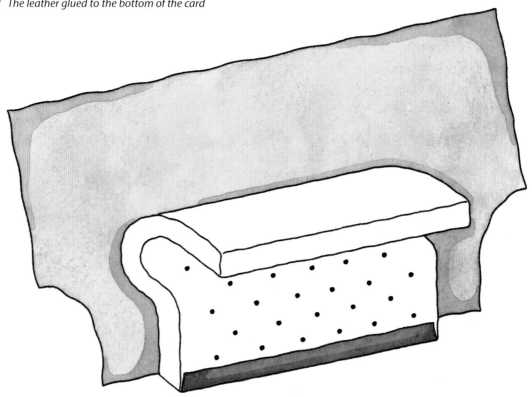

The 'buttoning'

1 The next stage is the 'buttoning'. To create this, first thread the needle with a double strand of waxed thread.

2 Push the needle into the bottom row, the left-hand black dot and foam, and through to the front of the leather.

3 Make a small stitch by inserting the needle $\frac{1}{16}$ in (1.5mm) from its exit point, then take the needle through to the back.

4 Pull the thread gently and tie off. Do not cut the thread. It is a good idea to press your finger on the stitch at the front while you tie off the thread, as this will result in a deeper button.

5 Move to the next dot on the right and repeat steps 3 and 4. Continue until all of the dots have a stitch through them, then fasten off securely. To prevent the leather from being stretched, ease it away from the foam as each row is completed. This will also help to form folds at each stitch and improve the final appearance of the buttoning.

6 Fold in the excess leather at each curved side and glue down. Do not stretch the leather while doing this (see Fig 12, below).

7 Glue the covered liner to the inside back of the sofa and push a pin into each bottom corner to hold the padding in place while the glue dries. Try not to pin into a visible part of the leather (see Fig 13, below).

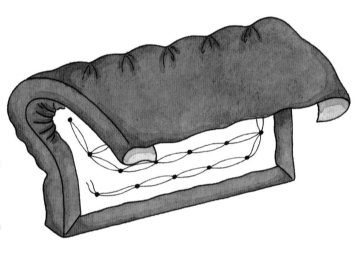

Fig 12 *After stitching the 'buttons', turn in the leather at the sides and glue it in position*

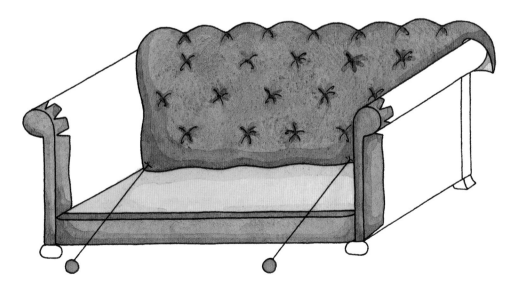

Fig 13 *Push a long pin into each corner, to hold the covered padding*

Fig 14 *The leather glued to the back curve*

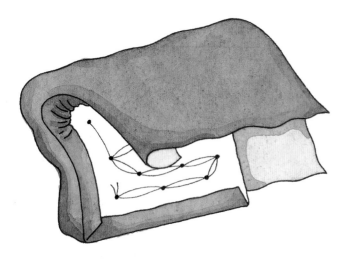

The sides

Due to the addition of padding and leather to the back, the inner sides will now be too wide to fit. Do not trim them until the leather is buttoned, because you would then have difficulty lining up the sewn dots when the sides are fitted.

1 'Button' the leather sides in the same manner as the back (see previous page).

2 Fold over and glue the excess leather at the back curved edge, notching the leather, if necessary, to help it to fold under smoothly (see Fig 14, left).

3 Try-fit the sides (i.e. do not use glue), pushing them firmly into the back corner. Trim off any card overlap but do not trim the foam. Remove the sides from the sofa (see Fig 15, below).

Fig 15 *Dry-fit (no glue) the side to trim the excess card*

4 Fold over the leather on the front straight edges. Do not stretch the leather, but ease in any fullness by pinching the leather into triangles on the underside of the card. Trim off the excess when the glue is dry (see Fig 16, right).

5 Glue the sides in position, pushing them firmly into the back corners. Hold in place, with pins unobtrusively placed in the front and back corners, until the glue is dry (see Fig 17, below). If any glue oozes out of the front arms, wipe it off immediately with a damp sponge.

Completing the 'buttoning'

1 For this stage you need your painted pins. Start at the bottom row of stitches on the padding covering the back of the seat, and push one of the pins through each stitch position, through the wood of the frame and out through the back of the sofa. Use flat-bladed pliers to help you to grip the pins and push them through, or use a pin-pusher if you have one (see page 5).

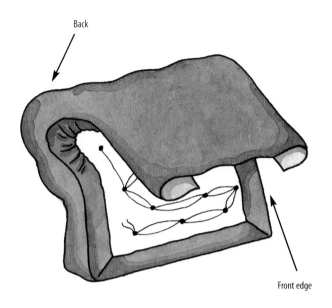

Back

Front edge

Fig 16 Easing the leather into triangles

Fig 17 The sides glued in position

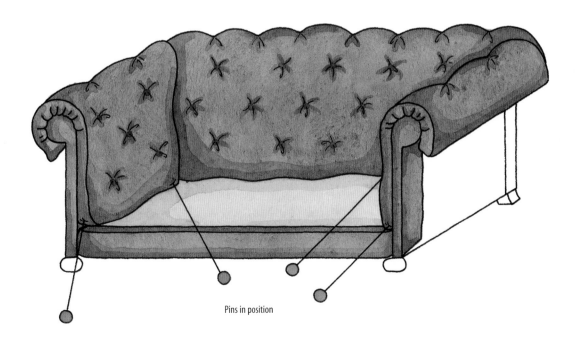

Pins in position

45

2 On the outside back, grip the pin close to the wood with the pliers, pull firmly and bend the pin over. The ends of the pliers may cause a depression in the wood at the back; if so, turn the pin so that it sits in the depression. The pins will not be seen when the back liner is in position. Repeat with all the stitch positions.

3 The top row of pins on the back and side rolls should be pushed in vertically.

4 Repeat on both of the sides.

Finishing off

1 Lightly hold down the leather on the back of the sofa, curving it over the back roll, then trim back to within ½in (12mm) of the underside of the roll.

2 Repeat step 1 with the leather on both sides.

3 Run a line of glue under the top roll at the back. Using the flat-bladed tool, and starting at the centre back, force the leather into the arm-roll join,

working outwards to each corner. Do not over-stretch the leather or you will lose the softness and buttoning on the top edge.

4 When the corner is reached, trim away as much excess leather as possible before forcing it into the joins, and take the leather to just around the corners.

5 Do the same with each side arm, starting at the front and working towards the back top corners, trimming and easing any thickness.

Fig 18 *The covered right and left side liners*

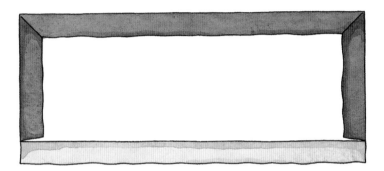

Fig 19 *The covered back liner*

Completing the outer back and sides

Use the back and side templates 'B' and 'C' (on page 34) to make the liners for the outer back and sides.

1 Place the back liner against the back of the sofa and, tucking it close to the underside of the back roll, trim to size along both the side edges and the bottom edge.

2 Remove the card from the sofa and trim a further ⅛in (3mm) from each side edge.

3 Repeat with both side liners but, with them, omit the extra ⅛in (3mm) trim.

4 Cut two pieces of thin leather ¼in (6mm) wider than the templates.

5 Repeat steps 1, 2 and 4 with the back liner.

6 Glue the card templates to the leather pieces.

7 On the side parts fold over and glue down the excess leather at the top and front edges only (Fig 18, above).

8 On the back card liner, fold over and glue down the excess leather on the top and both side edges (Fig 19).

9 Glue the side covers in position and glue the excess around the corner to the back of the sofa.

10 Trim the overhang at the back bottom corners.

11 Using the flat-bladed tool rub along the front edges to flatten the seam.

Fig 20

12 Glue on the back liner and rub the back side edges to flatten the joins.

13 Fold under the excess leather at the bottom edges and trim around the legs. Glue in position (see Fig 20, above).

14 Cut a piece of fabric to fit the base around the inside edges of the legs, and to cover the raw edges of the leather. Glue in position.

Cushions

Use the template, right, to make two cushions (see instructions on page 9). Remember to flip over the template in the direction of the arrow.

Finally, buff the sofa with a soft cloth, and it is complete.

Cushion template (actual size)

Knole-style Settee

This elegant settee is straightforward to construct, particularly if you have made any of the other projects in this book. The original Knole settee, which this project is based on, dates from the early seventeenth century and can still be seen at Knole House, in southern England. It is characterized by its high back and adjustable ends, and is perfect for that country-house look.

Materials and Equipment (see page 55, also, for upholstery)

Thin card for templates

$^1/_{16}$ in (1.5mm) plywood light

Heavy mount board

$^3/_8$ x $^1/_{16}$ in (9 x 1.5mm) pine strip wood

$^7/_8$ x $^1/_4$ in (21 x 6mm) balsa strip (it can be bought in this size, or cut from $^1/_4$ in/6mm balsa sheet)

$^1/_4$ in (6mm) square hardwood (jelutong is most suitable)

2 turned feet or the round ends from two newel posts, or the round ends from two dolly pegs

1 cocktail stick for use as dowels

Wood glue

A

Back

B

Seat

Note

For correct size this template should be enlarged by 111%

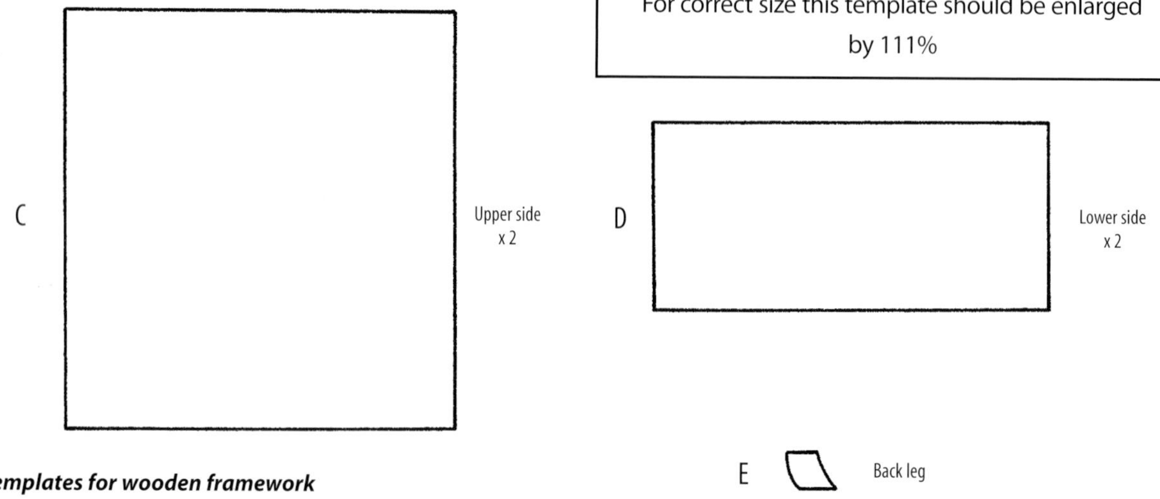

C

Upper side
x 2

D

Lower side
x 2

Templates for wooden framework

E   Back leg

Layout (not to scale)

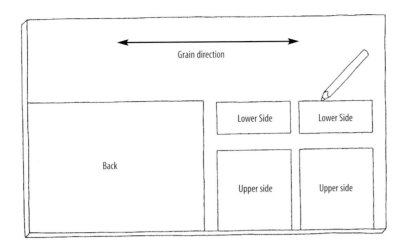

The fabric I have used is an ordinary dress-weight velvet and a computer-printed woven fabric. The settee would look less heavy with a thinner velvet, but I like the soft cosiness of this look. If you do not have access to a computer and printer, the settee would look equally nice in a subtle, all-over design.

Construction

I have used a thin plywood for the back and sides and reinforced it with mount board, which adds thickness and strength without affecting the overall dimensions (the side will not fit if the wood is thicker).

Enlarge templates 'A', 'C' and 'D' (on facing page) by 111%, photocopy or trace onto thin card, and cut out. Photocopy or trace template 'F', below, onto thin card.

1 Lay the back and side templates 'C' and 'D' on plywood light, as shown in the diagram above. Draw around the shapes, then cut them out.

2 Take the two lower side and two upper side templates 'C' and 'D' again, and lay them, together with the inner back liner template 'F' below, on mount board. Draw around the shapes and cut out.

Template for the inner back liner (actual size)

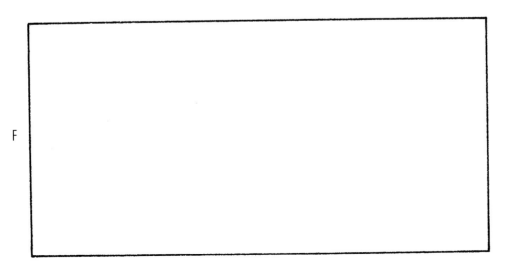

Fig 1 The lower seat base

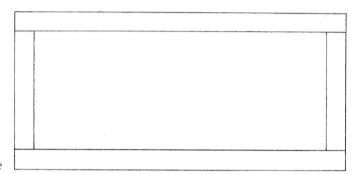

Fig 2 The upper seat base

3 Glue the four plywood light side parts to the four mount board side parts, place them under a heavy weight and allow the glue to dry.

4 Use sandpaper to smooth and even up the edges of the side parts, then set aside until needed.

5 From $^3/_8$ x $^1/_{16}$in (9 x 1.5mm) pine strip wood cut two pieces 4$^7/_8$in (122mm) long, and two pieces 1$^3/_8$in (35mm) long, for the lower seat base.

6 From $^7/_8$ x $^1/_4$in (21 x 6mm) balsa strip wood cut two pieces 4$^7/_8$in long and 2 pieces 1$^3/_4$in (44mm) long for the upper seat base.

7 Lay out and glue the parts cut in step 5, referring to Fig 1 above. It will help to do this on waxed paper, to prevent them sticking to your work surface.

8 Repeat the process with the parts cut in step 6, referring to Fig 2 above.

9 To form the seat base, glue the parts from step 8 on top of the parts from step 7 (see Fig 3, top diagram, on the facing page). Place a weight on top until the glue is dry, then sand the front corners to round them off.

10 Glue the large plywood back part A to the back of the seat base, lining up the bottom and side edges (see Fig 4, middle diagram on the facing page).

11 Glue the smaller side parts D to each end of the seat base, wood-side outermost, as shown in Fig 5 (bottom diagram, facing page).

12 Glue the mount board panel from step 2 to the inside surface of the back panel attached to the seat base.

13 Draw around the back leg template E onto the two opposing sides of the $^1/_4$in (6mm) square hardwood strip. Shape the front and back leg curves with a knife, then cut the leg free from the strip wood and repeat the procedure for the second leg.

Fig 3 The seat base

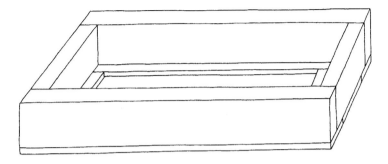

14 Drill a hole in the tops of the legs, using a drill bit the same diameter as the cocktail stick. Snip the tapered end from the stick and discard it. Dip the cut end into a little wood glue and insert into the hole drilled in the top of one of the legs. Snip free the rest of the stick leaving ¼in (6mm) behind. Repeat on the other back leg.

15 Drill the tops of the turned front feet, then dowel in the same way as the back legs, as described in the previous step.

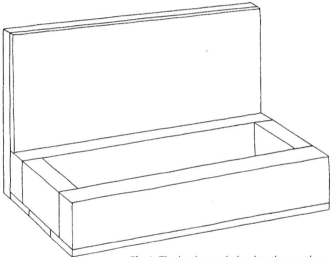

Fig 4 The back panel glued to the seat base

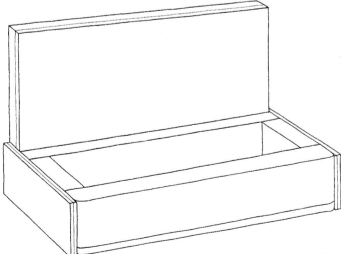

Fig 5 Glue on the side parts. Note that the corners of the seat base have been slightly rounded

16 Mark the position for the leg attachment on the
base of the seat assembly, $1/4$in (6mm) in from each
direction at each corner. Do not include the side
panels in the measurement, measure only the seat
base. Drill the holes $1/4$in (6mm) deep.

17 Stain and varnish the legs and feet using your
chosen method.

The wooden framework

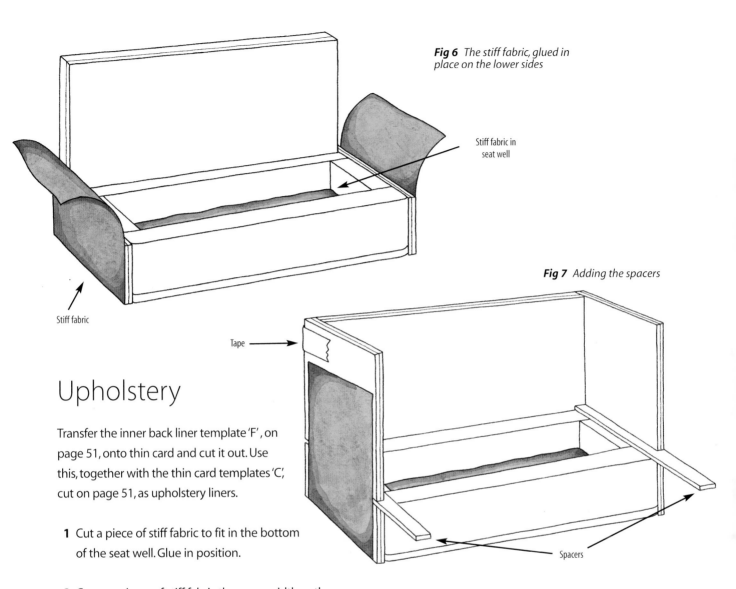

Fig 6 *The stiff fabric, glued in place on the lower sides*

Stiff fabric in seat well

Fig 7 *Adding the spacers*

Tape

Stiff fabric

Spacers

Upholstery

Transfer the inner back liner template 'F', on page 51, onto thin card and cut it out. Use this, together with the thin card templates 'C', cut on page 51, as upholstery liners.

1 Cut a piece of stiff fabric to fit in the bottom of the seat well. Glue in position.

2 Cut two pieces of stiff fabric the same width as the side panels and 2in (48mm) high. Glue half of the fabric to the small side panel that is attached to the base (see Fig 6, above). Cut two scraps of any ⅛in (3mm) thick wood about 2–3in (48–72mm) long, to act as spacers when attaching the larger side panels.

3 Position a spacer on top of one of the small side panels. Spread a thin layer of glue on the lower ½in (12mm) of the wood side of the large side panel. Sit the panel on the spacer, card-side innermost, and press the remaining fabric onto the glue. Do not get glue on the spacer, or you may not get it out again. Tape in position, keeping the upper panel level with the lower, and leave taped up until the glue is dry (see Fig 7, above right). Repeat on the second side.

For the upholstery you will need:

Main fabric
Dried silver sand (see page 4)
Small quantity of wadding (batting)
Mighty tack glue
Sewing needle and matching thread
4 tassels and cording for ties
4 turned posts. I used the end part from 2 tiny, ready-dowelled turnings, which are commercially made strips of miniature turned parts intended to be cut apart and used
¼in (6mm) or less thick foam
Square of stiff fabric (see page 7)

Fig 8 *The sides opened out*

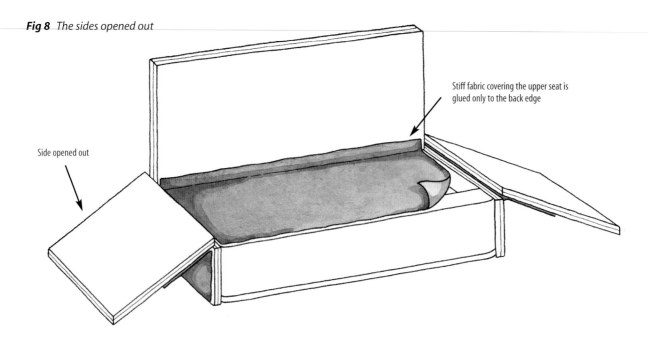

Stiff fabric covering the upper seat is glued only to the back edge

Side opened out

4 Remove the spacers and tape. Cut a piece of stiff fabric large enough to cover the seat surface (see Fig 8, above). Glue in position only along the back edge.

5 Cut a piece of your main fabric long enough to cover the front of the seat base (but not the edges of the side panels) and 1in (24mm) wider than the depth of the seat. Glue the fabric to the front of

the seat base, so that there is a ¹⁄₂in (12mm) overhang top and bottom (see Fig 9, below). Push the edges of the fabric between the seat base and the side panel.

6 Spread glue on the reverse of the fabric that is overhanging the top of the seat surface, then fold down the glued fabric onto the top of the seat base.

Fig 9 *Adding the fabric to the front of the seat*

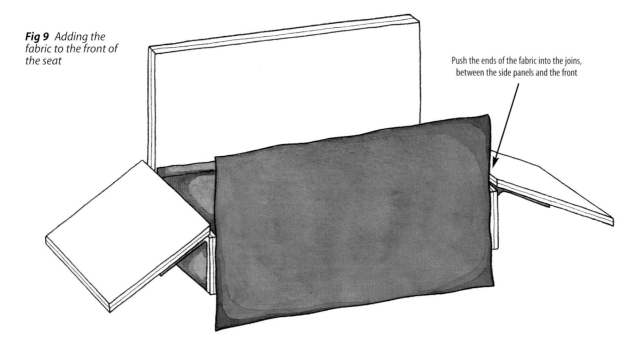

Push the ends of the fabric into the joins, between the side panels and the front

Fig 10

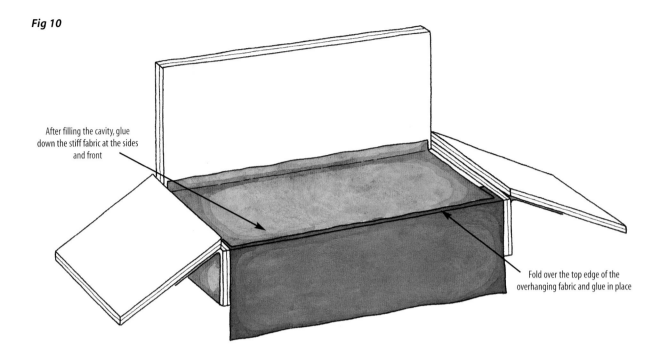

After filling the cavity, glue down the stiff fabric at the sides and front

Fold over the top edge of the overhanging fabric and glue in place

7 Cover the inside of the seat well with a ¹⁄₄in (6mm) layer of dried sand. Pack out the rest of the space with wadding (batting). Trim the front edge of the stiff fabric glued to the back of the seat so that there is ¹⁄₄in (6mm) of main fabric exposed. Spread glue on the three remaining edges of the stiff fabric, making sure that it gets right up to the front edge and there is at least a ¹⁄₄in (6mm) wide band of glue. Press the stiff fabric down on to the seat surface and immediately wipe off any glue that oozes out (see Fig 10, above). Do not get any glue on the main fabric.

8 Trim the overhanging main fabric at the bottom edge of the seat, so that it fits around the front legs. Glue the fabric in position.

9 Cut a piece of main fabric ¹⁄₂in (12mm) wider all around than the whole side panel, including the small panel glued to the base (see Fig 11, right). Spread glue all over both side parts and centre the fabric over them. Press in position.

10 With the sofa facing you, snip the fabric level with the seat and trim the lower piece to fit into the same groove as the seat front fabric, glue in place (see Fig 11, below).

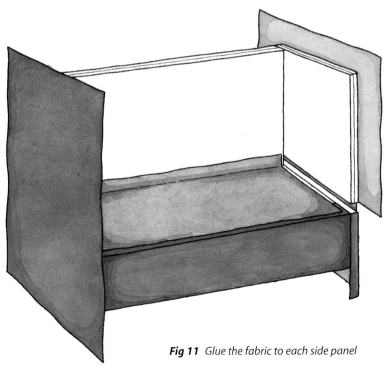

Fig 11 Glue the fabric to each side panel

Fig 12 *Fold and glue the excess fabric to the back edge of the sofa at the two bottom edges*

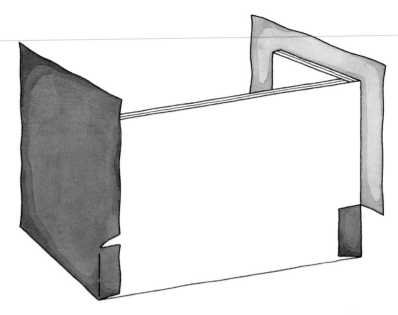

11 Turn the sofa so that the back is facing towards you and snip the fabric level with the seat, as in the previous step, but this time take the excess lower fabric around to the back (see Fig 12, above).

12 Spread glue on the wrong side of the overhanging fabric (rather than on the wood) and fold the fabric over to the inside of the side panels. Do not overlap the fabric at the corners, but pinch the corners together tightly to form a triangle. Cut the triangle off, so that the fabric is automatically mitred, (see Fig 13, below).

13 Trim the fabric at the bottom edge to fit around the feet and legs and glue to the underside of the sofa.

14 Repeat steps 9–13 on the other side and the back.

15 Trim the inner back upholstery liner to fit inside the back. Cut the liner so that it is $1/8$in (3mm) shorter than the back at each end and $1/4$in (6mm) below the top edge of the back.

16 Cut a piece of foam to exactly the same size as the liner. Glue the foam to the card.

Fig 13 *Fold over and glue the excess fabric to the inside of the upper side panels*

17 Cut a piece of fabric ¹/₂in (12mm) larger all around than the card/foam liner.

18 Centre the foam side of the liner on the reverse of the fabric. Fold over the excess fabric at each edge and glue to the back of the card, mitring the corners as you did with the side panels (Fig 14, right). Set aside.

19 Make up the inner side panels in the same way, but this time trim the card so that there is ¹/₄in (6mm) of the main fabric exposed at the back of the side panel as well as at the top edge; ¹/₈in (3mm) is enough allowance at the front edge. Set aside.

20 Before fitting the padded panels, open out the side panels and add a small folded piece of stiff fabric or main fabric into the join, as shown in Fig 15 below. Do not omit this, or there will be an obvious gap in the upholstery and, if done incorrectly the side panel will not open.

21 Glue on the back and side panels, allowing a gap of ¹/₄in (6mm) at the inside back when you fit them. If you omit this gap then the side panels will not close up properly.

22 Next, drill holes to take the dowels on the base of the four turned top posts. Using a drill bit the same size as the dowels, drill through the fabric ³/₈in (9mm) from each top end of the back panel. Drill a hole the same distance from the back of each side panel. To help you to find the drilled holes again, pop a little bit of cocktail stick in each hole to mark its position. (See pictures overleaf, showing the posts in position.)

Fig 14

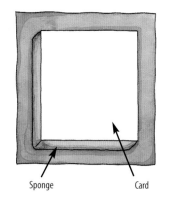

Fold over the excess fabric and glue it to the back of the card

Sponge   Card

23 Stain and varnish each post before gluing into the drill holes.

24 Make the cushions, either one single or two smaller ones, using the seat base template 'B' on page 50 as a template, and following the instructions for making cushions given on page 9.

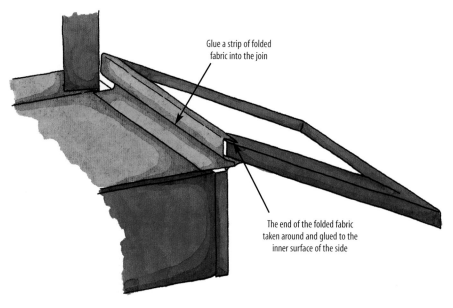

Glue a strip of folded fabric into the join

The end of the folded fabric taken around and glued to the inner surface of the side

Fig 15 The fabric must fold into the join in this manner

To complete the settee, tie a twisted cord with tassels around the two top posts on each of the side and back corners. If you wish to make the settee even more sumptuous, you could add extra cushions.

Leather Club Suite

I am not exactly sure when this comfortable suite dates from but it was certainly around in the early 1920s, when the armchairs could be found in many gentlemen's clubs and libraries, and the whole suite could be found in the best parlours of middle-class homes.

Materials and Equipment

Thin card for templates

$1/4$ in (6mm) jelutong or balsa sheet

$3/8$ in (9mm) balsa dowel

10 x 2mm pine strip (only sold in metric)

$3/8$ x $1/4$ in (9 x 6mm) jelutong or balsa strip

$1/16$ in (1.5mm) plywood light, or heavy mount board

Dried silver sand (see page 4)

6 bun feet, either commercially made, the round ends from 6 newel posts, or the round ends from 6 wooden dolly pegs

6 back legs as template, cut from $1/4$ in (6mm) square hardwood (not balsa)

Wood glue

Waxed paper (optional)

Stiff fabric for lining (see page 7)

Large-headed pins or small clamps (sash type)

Piece of brown leather, approximately 4sq. ft (120cm^2) plus an extra matched piece of leather, in case it is needed

Leather glue

$1/2$ in and $1/4$ in (12mm and 6mm) foam sheet approx. 12in (30cm) square

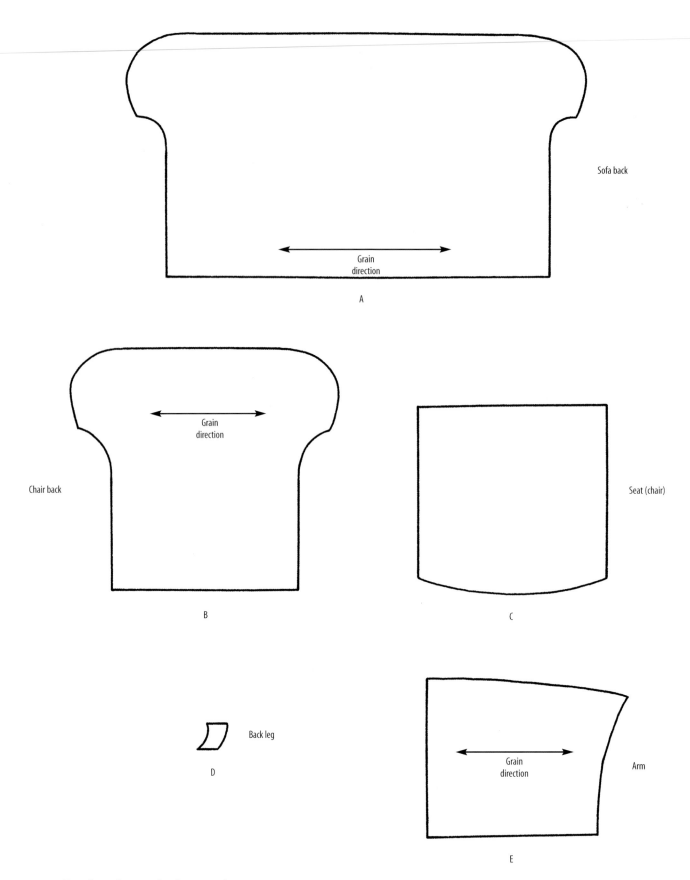

Sofa back

Grain
direction

A

Chair back

Grain
direction

B

Seat (chair)

C

Back leg

D

Grain
direction

Arm

E

Templates for wooden framework

Template for the sofa seat

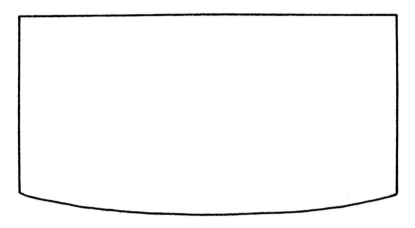

F

Constructing the sofa base

First, photocopy, scan or trace the templates onto thin card.

1 From the 10 x 2mm pine strip, cut two pieces 4in (100mm) long and two pieces 1¼in (30mm) long for the lower seat base.

2 Glue the pine strips just cut in position, as shown in Fig 1, above right. Wipe off any glue that oozes out, and allow to dry completely.

3 From the ⅜ x ¼in (9 x 6mm) jelutong or balsa strip, cut two pieces 4in (100mm) long and two 1½in (36mm) long for the upper seat base.

4 Glue together these pieces as shown in Fig 2, bottom right. Again, wipe off surplus glue.

Tip
Place waxed paper underneath when gluing, to prevent wood sticking to your work surface.

Fig 1 *Layout for the lower seat base (not to scale)*

Fig 2 *Layout for the upper seat base (not to scale)*

5 Glue the upper seat base on top of the lower seat base, lining up the sides and back exactly (see Figs 3 and 4). Place a weight, such as a book, on top of the parts until the glue has dried.

6 Place the sofa seat template 'F' on top of the seat base just constructed, and draw the curvature on the front rail. Cut to shape with a hand or electric fretsaw and sand smooth.

7 Draw around the sofa back shape, template 'A', onto $1/16$in (1.5mm) plywood light, or heavy mount board, then cut out the shape. If you are using plywood, the template must be in the same direction as the grain. Mount board has a grain, too: the board will only curve without creasing in one direction. Since it is necessary for the back to curve, you will need to find out in which direction your mount board curves. Place the template so that the arrow runs in the same direction as the natural curve and not across it.

8 Glue the sofa back to the sofa base, lining up at the side and back edges. Allow to dry completely.

9 The chair seats and backs are constructed in exactly the same way.

Fig 3 The seat base, plan view

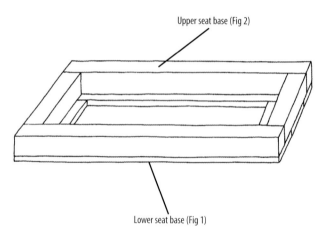

Fig 4 The seat base, side view

Fig 5 Seat base with back attached

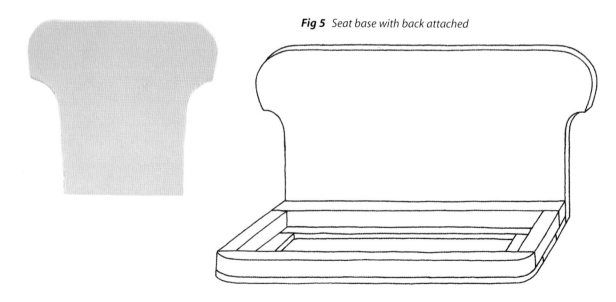

Fig 6 *Chair arm: cut six, for the sofa and two chairs*

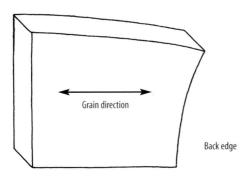

Grain direction

Back edge

The side and arm assembly

1 For the chair and sofa arms, draw around the side (arm) template onto ¼in (6mm) jelutong or balsa sheet six times, ensuring that the arrow is in the direction of the grain (see Fig 6, left). Cut out the six parts, and mark three right sides and three left sides.

2 For the rounded arms, cut six pieces of ³⁄₈in (9mm) balsa dowel, 2¹⁄₈in (51mm) long.

3 Flatten one side of each piece of dowel, each one to the same extent (see Fig 7, left).

4 Glue one piece of dowel to the top edge of each side part, again ensuring that you have three right sides and three left sides (see Fig 8, below left).

5 Using a craft knife and sandpaper, curve the top inside edge of the sides to match the curvature of the dowel (see Fig 9, below).

Fig 7 *Dowel: cut six*

Flatten on one side

Fig 8 *Glue the half dowels to the outside of each side part, making sure that you have three right and three left sides*

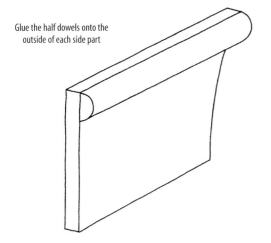

Glue the half dowels onto the outside of each side part

Fig 9 *Curving the inner top*

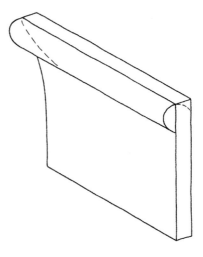

6 Shape the outer face of the dowel/arms, using a craft knife and sandpaper (see Fig 10, right).

7 On the inner side of each arm assembly, draw a line $^7/_{16}$in (11mm) from the bottom edge across the whole width of the side. $^1/_{16}$in (1.5mm) above this line draw a second line. With a craft knife and a metal ruler score each line $^1/_{16}$in (1.5mm) deep. Remove the wood between the lines (see Fig 11, lower right). You can use a craft knife for this but a better and more controlled result would be obtained using a $^1/_{16}$in (1.5mm) chisel. Alternatively (and probably more accurately), hold the side assembly against the side of the chair base, lining up the back and bottom edges. Draw the first line at this level, using the top edge of the seat as the straight edge and the second line $^1/_{16}$in (1.5mm) above this.

8 Sand level the front edge of each side assembly. You are now ready to begin the upholstery.

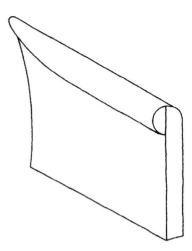

Fig 10 *Curving the outer back dowel*

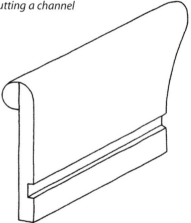

Fig 11 *Cutting a channel*

The wooden framework

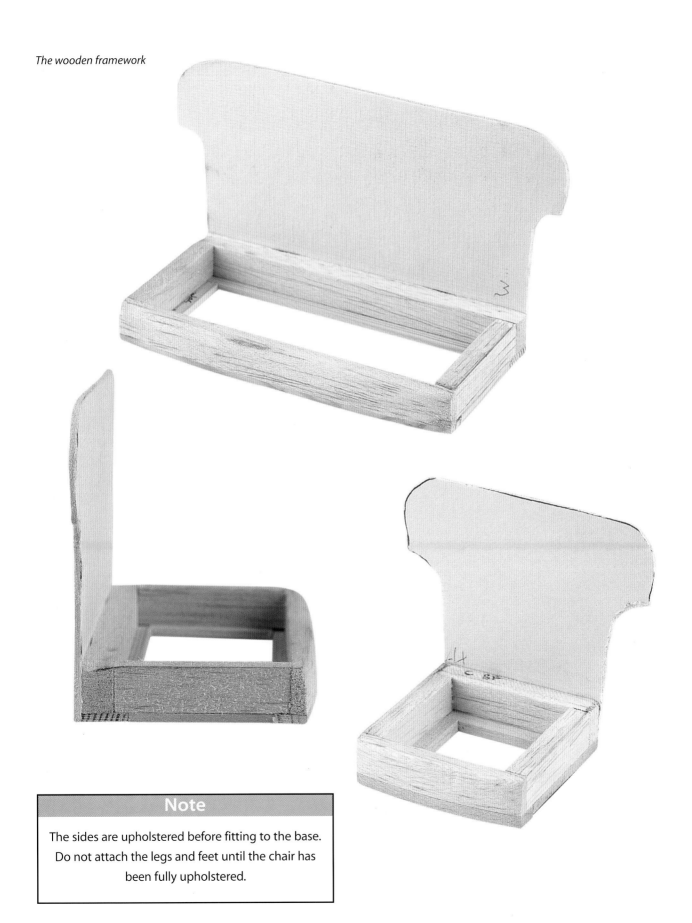

Note

The sides are upholstered before fitting to the base.
Do not attach the legs and feet until the chair has
been fully upholstered.

Templates for the liners

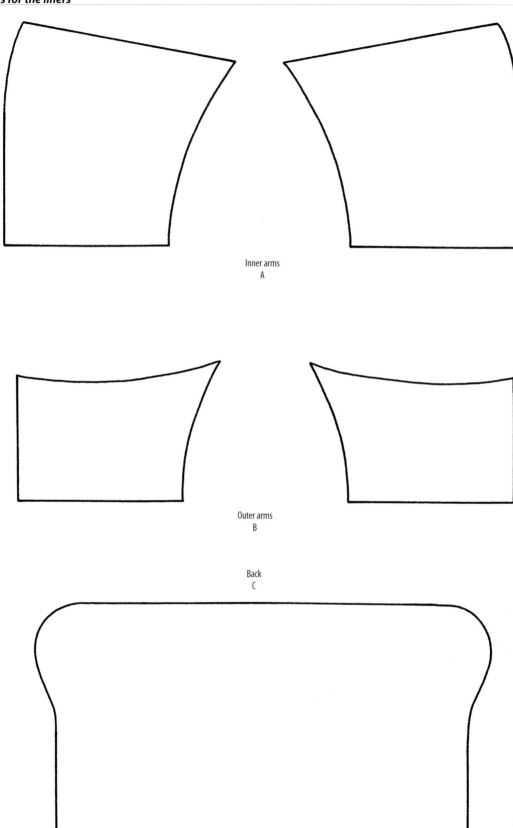

Inner arms
A

Outer arms
B

Back
C

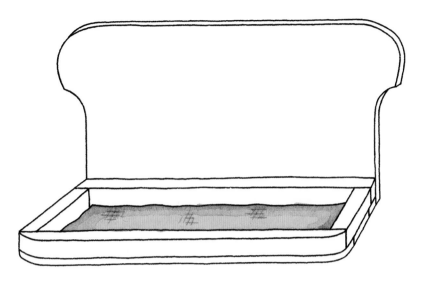

Fig 12 *Fabric fixed inside the well of the seat*

Upholstery

The procedure for upholstery is the same for all three pieces of the suite and the instructions will refer to any of the pieces.

1 Cut a piece of the closely woven stiff lining fabric to fit inside the seat well, glue in position, then coat with PVA glue (see Fig 12, above).

2 Cut a second piece of the stiff fabric to fit the top surface of the seat. Glue in position only along the back edge of the seat top, where the seat joins the back. Trim the front edge of the fabric a further $1/8$in (3mm) following the curvature of the chair (see Fig 13, below).

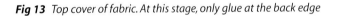

Fig 13 *Top cover of fabric. At this stage, only glue at the back edge*

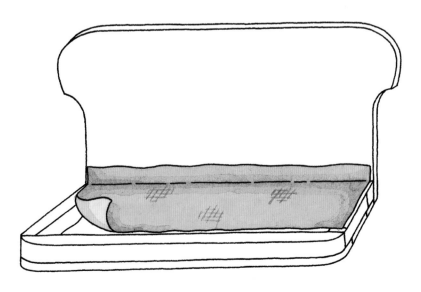

Fig 14 *Gluing the leather to the front rail*

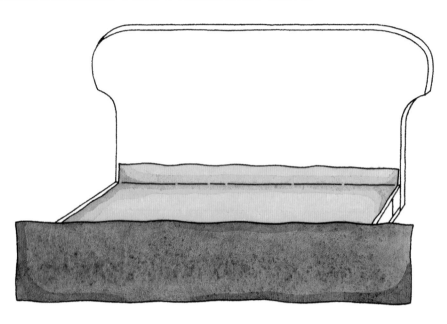

Fig 15 *The leather, trimmed, and stuck down*

3 Cut a piece of leather to cover the front curved rail of the chair, larger all around by at least ¹/₂in (12mm) – a thicker piece of leather can be used for this. Centre, then glue up the leather and press onto the front rail, smoothing and stretching as you go (see Fig 14, above).

4 Spread glue over the back of the leather that overhangs each edge. Smooth the leather down over the top of the front rail, the base of the front rail and at each side. Pinch the triangles in the leather that form at each corner – using a pair of flat-bladed pliers for this will form a tight, really close triangle. Leave the chair until the glue has dried, then cut off the triangles close to the chair (see Fig 15, right).

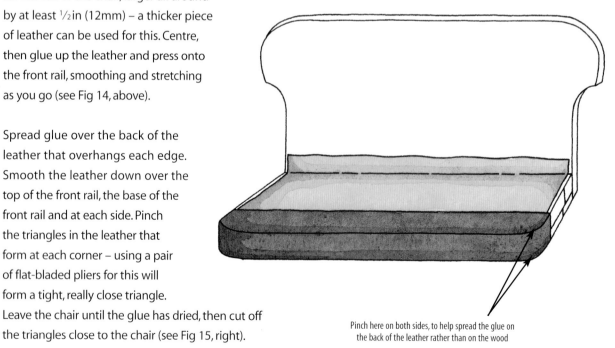

Pinch here on both sides, to help spread the glue on the back of the leather rather than on the wood

5 Fill the cavity with dried silver sand and glue down the fabric cover at the front and sides.

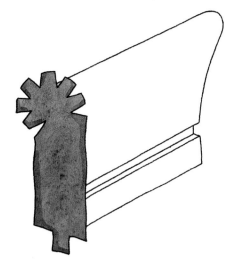

Fig 16 *Glue a piece of leather to the front of the arm*

6 Cut a piece of leather to cover the front flat face of the side assembly. The leather should be ½in (12mm) larger all around than the front of the arm. Glue in position on the front of the arm. Cut a notch in the leather where the arm roll meets the chair side, and trim the corners at the bottom (see Fig 16, right).

7 Spread glue over the reverse of the overhanging leather, but not on the piece overhanging at the bottom of the side. Smooth back the leather along both flat faces of the side, then ease the leather over the curved surface, pinching the excess into triangles as you go.

8 When the glue is dry, snip off the triangles to tidy up, then trim the leather away from the channel cut into the side assembly (see Fig 17, right).

The sides

1 Photocopy or trace the templates 'A' for the inner arm liners (see page 68) onto thin card. Cut out.

2 Try-fit the liners in position. They should fit from the channel cut on the inside surface of the side, up over the arm and around the arm roll. The liners will need to be trimmed at the (inside) back of the arm roll.

3 Using the liners as a template cut a piece of the thinner, ½in (12mm) foam to the width of the liner and at least 2in (48mm) longer. Trim a further ¼in (6mm) from the width of the foam at the back.

4 Glue the foam to the liner at the bottom straight edge, aligning the edges.

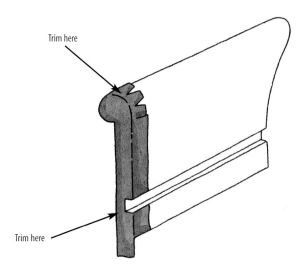

Trim here

Trim here

Fig 17 *Snip off the triangles to tidy up, then trim the leather away from the channel*

5 Pin the liner at the bottom straight edge in position, just above the channel cut into the inner side.

6 Spread glue over the rest of the liner, curve gently over the arm and pin in position. Very gently and without stretching it, curve the foam over the liner. Carefully remove the pins and re-insert them through the foam. This procedure will prevent the foam from being stretched and thus flattened when the leather is applied.

7 When the liner/foam is dry, remove it from the arm assembly and use it as a template to cut the leather. The leather should be at least 1in (24mm) larger all around than the liner. Curve the leather over the liner before cutting, to make sure that it is long enough.

8 Run a line of glue into the channel cut into the inner side of the arm assembly. Using your flat-bladed blunt tool, push the bottom edge of the leather piece into the channel. There must be a ¹⁄₂ in (12mm) overhang at the front edge of the side part. You must allow the glue to dry completely at this point, otherwise the leather joint will not withstand the pulling necessary at the next stage (see Fig 18, right).

9 Insert the liner/foam between the side and the leather. Make sure that the liner is as close as possible to the join between the leather and wood (see Fig 19, below). Also make sure that the front straight edge of the liner is level with the front edge of the arm assembly.

Fig 18 *Push the leather into the groove*

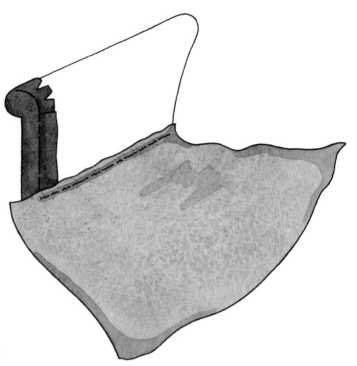

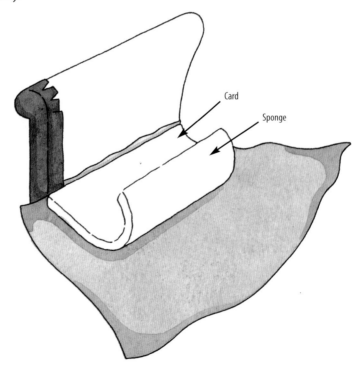

Fig 19 *Inserting the foam between the side and the leather*

Fig 20 *Gluing the excess leather to the card*

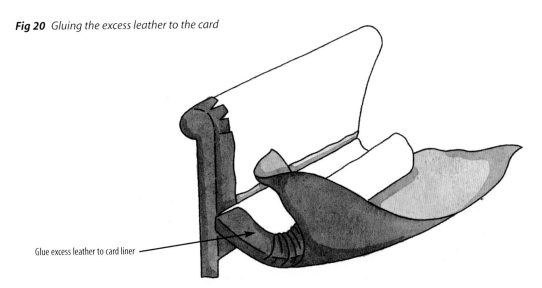

Glue excess leather to card liner

Fig 21 *Glue the card/leather to the side*

Trim here

Push excess leather into
the join

10 Turn over and glue the excess leather to the card liner at the front straight edge (see Fig 20, above).

11 Glue the leather/foam/liner sandwich to the side and over the arm roll. Pin in place until the glue dries (see Fig 21, left). Immediately wipe off any glue that oozes out at the front with a damp sponge.

12 When the glue is dry, trim back any overhanging foam and card until it is just above the join line of the underside of the dowel and side part. Trim back the excess leather until it fits neatly underneath the arm roll, with a tiny bit to spare. Run a line of glue underneath the arm roll at the join between roll and side and, using your flat-bladed tool push the excess leather into the join (see Fig 22, below).

Fig 22 *Gluing the leather to the arm roll*

Fig 23 *Draw around the back shape onto the sponge, then cut to shape*

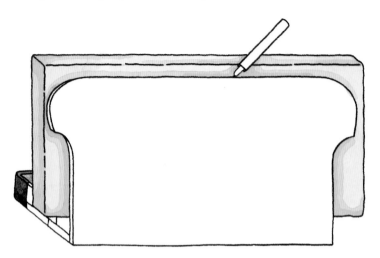

Fig 23 *Draw around the back shape onto the sponge, then cut to shape*

The back

1 Lay the back template 'A' or 'B' flat on the back of the leather and draw around it. Add 1½in (36mm) allowance all around the drawn line and cut out on the allowance line.

2 Place a piece of foam against the front surface of the back attached to the chair, and using a ballpoint pen draw around the back shape. Cut the foam exactly on the line (see Fig 23, above).

3 Trim the bottom front edge of the foam to a curve.

4 Glue the leather piece cut in step 1 to the back of the chair seat (see Fig 24, below). Allow to dry before proceeding.

5 Position the foam prepared in steps 2 and 3 against the inside back. Lift up the leather over the foam and smooth out.

Fig 24 *Leather glued along the back edge*

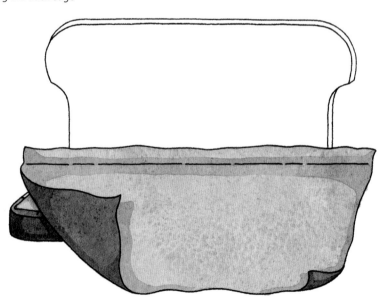

Fig 25 *Slitting and notching the leather at the back*

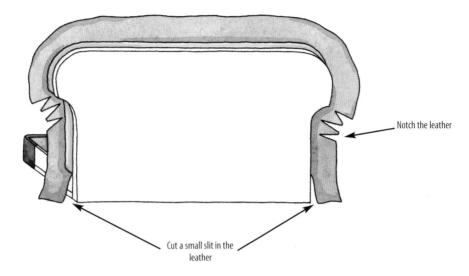

Notch the leather

Cut a small slit in the
leather

6 Hold the leather in position with one hand while you cut a small slit in the leather fold either side of the base at the back. Still holding the leather in place, cut notches around the side position curves on each side of the back (see Fig 25, above).

7 Spread glue on the reverse of the leather overhanging the back. Fold over both sides, easing the previously notched leather around the underarm curves. Then, with the back of the chair facing you, bring the leather down over the top back edge and, working from the centre out to each side, stretch and glue down the leather, forming triangles to take in the excess over the curves (see Fig 26, below).

8 Trim off the triangles when the glue is dry.

Fig 26 *Glue the excess leather to the back*

Fig 27 The arms in position

Attaching the sides

Before attaching the sides to the chair, very carefully pull the back outwards into a gentle curve. It will spring back but that doesn't matter, this initial pulling will release some of the stiffness and tension. Obviously do not pull so hard that the back bends or, worse still, comes away from the seat base, as the object is to add a gentle curve to the back.

1 Spread wood glue on both sides of the chair and up the sides of the back as far as the curve.

Fig 28 The card glued to the liner and the corners cut out

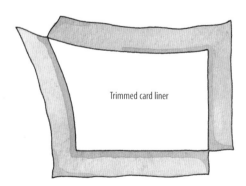

Trimmed card liner

2 Position the side-arm assembly against the chair side, making sure that the seat bottom and the side bottom edges are exactly level, and also that the back of the arm assembly is level with the back of the chair (see Fig 27, above). When both sides are in position pull the back to the same curvature as the back of the sides, and clamp in position. Allow to dry completely before removing the clamps.

The outer covers

1 Photocopy or trace the outer arm liners 'B' on page 68 onto thin card. Cut out the shapes.

2 Try-fit the liners onto the outer sides. They should fit from the front straight edge to the back curve with no excess. They should also fit closely under the curvature of the arm roll and $\frac{1}{8}$in (3mm) above the bottom edge.

3 Cut a piece of leather $\frac{1}{2}$in (12mm) larger all around than the card liner. Centre and glue the liner to the reverse of the leather, making sure that you have a left and a right side liner.

4 Cut the corners out of the leather (see Fig 28, left).

5 Glue down the leather to the reverse of the card at the front and top edges, mitring the front corner by pinching the leather into a triangle and cutting it off (see Fig 29, right).

6 Glue the liner in position, lining up the front edges and under the arm. Wipe off any excess glue with a damp sponge. Using the flat face of your tool rub the front edge join firmly, to give a neat, close finish.

7 Spread glue over the leather overhang at the side back and, taking the leather around to the rear of the chair, stick down.

8 Spread glue over the leather overhang at the bottom edge and also the small overhang at the bottom front, then fold under the leather, mitring it at the front (see Fig 30, below). Trim away the triangle formed at the underside front.

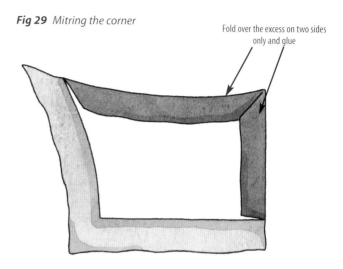

Fig 29 *Mitring the corner*

Fold over the excess on two sides only and glue

Adding the back

1 Photocopy or trace the back liner template on page 68 onto thin card, and cut it out.

2 Try-fit the liner onto the back of the chair, trimming off any excess as necessary; the liner should not overhang any side of the chair.

3 Cut a piece of leather $\frac{1}{2}$ in (12mm) larger on all sides than the liner.

Fig 30 *The side liner in position*

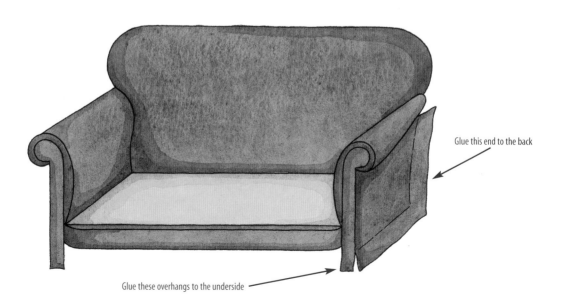

Glue this end to the back

Glue these overhangs to the underside

4 Centre the liner on the back of the leather and glue in position (see Fig 31, right).

5 Cut out the bottom two corners (see Fig 31, right) and spread glue around the overhanging leather; glue the leather to the reverse of the card on three sides only (see Fig 32, below right). Do not glue down the leather overhanging the bottom straight edge.

6 Spread glue on the reverse of the back liner, making sure that it goes right up to the edges.

7 Position the liner on the back of the chair. Wipe off any excess glue and use the flat-bladed tool to firmly rub the edges.

8 Fold under the excess leather at the bottom edge and glue in position on the under side of the chair (see Fig 33, below). Set aside until the glue is dry.

Fig 31 The leather glued to the card

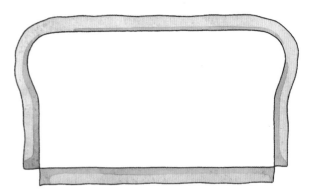

Fig 32 The overhanging excess leather glued to the back of the card

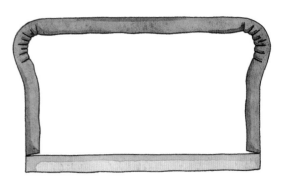

Fig 33 The covered back liner in position

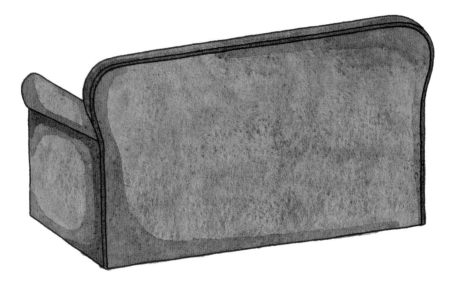

Attaching the legs

1 Measure ¹/₄ in (6mm) in from each corner and drill a hole deep enough to take the leg dowels.

2 Using a sharp craft knife cut away the leather around each drill hole to a distance ¹/₁₆ in (1.5mm).

3 Glue in the legs and feet. A bun foot in each front corner and a leg in each back corner. Varnish or colour as desired.

4 Cut a piece of stiff fabric large enough to cover the edges of the leather on the underside of the seat, trim around the inside curves of the bun feet and the inside corners of the back legs. Glue the liner in position.

The cushions

Use seat base templates 'C' and 'F' (on pages 62 and 63) as templates for the cushions, but trim ¹/₈ in (3mm) from all sides. Make up the cushions following the instructions given in the introductory chapter (see page 9).

To complete the suite, polish with your chosen leather polish. I used boot polish for this example.

Three Chaises Longues

The chaise longue, which is also known as a day bed, has been around for many centuries. Traditionally, it was used for resting and relaxing during the day, often when recovering from a malaise or from the excesses of the night before.

Materials and Equipment

Thin card for templates and liners

$1/4$ x $3/8$ in (6 x 9mm) balsa or jelutong strip

$1/16$ x $3/8$ in (1.5 x 9mm) pine or jelutong strip (not balsa)

$1/4$ in (6mm) balsa or jelutong sheet

$1/2$ in or $3/8$ in (12mm or 9mm) balsa dowel

PVA glue

Cocktail sticks for dowels

4 cabriole legs, no higher than $3/4$ in (18mm)

Stiff fabric for lining

Dry sand (see page 4)

$1/2$ in (12mm) foam

Small piece of thin wadding (batting), preferably cotton

Stiff lining fabric for base liners (see page 7)

Fine velvets for upholstery (see 'Notes' on pages 81 and 88)

Sewing needles for fabric and leather

Thread to match fabrics and leather

Stain, polish, or paint for the legs

Trimmings: tassels and fringes for the first chaise longue (see page 93)

Velvet-covered Chaise Longue

It is primarily the fabric that will give an indication of the period and the Victorians tended to use leather and heavier velvets. A larger chaise longue, called a divan, which was upholstered using fine imported rugs in both flat and woven pile, was also fashionable and this is the first type of chaise longue described. As you can see, there was no wood showing on the divan and it was heavily upholstered, with fringes and tassels down to the floor.

The basic construction of each of these chaises longues is exactly the same. For this reason I will detail the construction and upholstery for one and only give the instructions for any variation in

construction and upholstery for the other two. I will start with the velvet-covered chaise, which has the basic structure without any adaptation. This chaise is full of eastern promise and so perhaps I should have called it Turkish Delight.

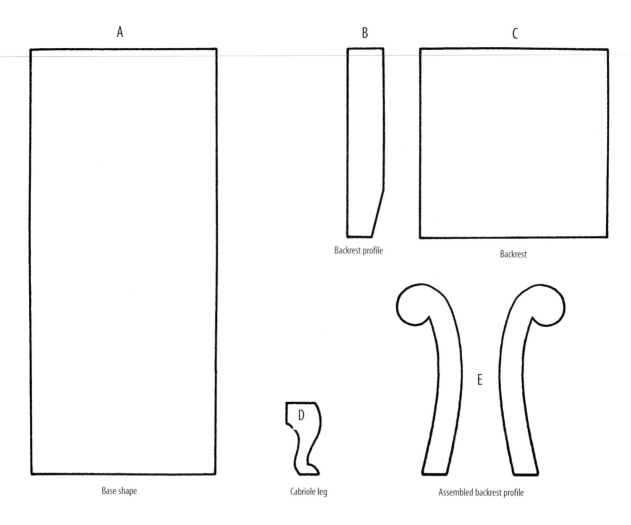

A

Base shape

B

Backrest profile

C

Backrest

D

Cabriole leg

E

Assembled backrest profile

Templates for the wooden framework

Constructing the wooden framework

Photocopy or trace the templates onto thin card.

1 For the upper seat base, cut two pieces of $^1/_4$ x $^3/_8$ in (6 x 9mm) jelutong or balsa strip 4$^3/_8$in (109mm) long, and two strips 1$^1/_2$in (36mm) long.

2 For the lower seat base, cut two pieces of $^1/_{16}$ x $^3/_8$ in (1.5 x 9mm) pine strip 4$^3/_8$in (109mm) long, and cut two pieces 1$^1/_4$in (30mm) long.

3 Make up the upper and lower seat bases following the Fig 1 diagrams on the facing page. Glue the upper base on top of the lower base, then leave to dry under a heavy weight, such as a book.

4 Cut out the backrest (template 'C', above) from the balsa or jelutong sheet (see Fig 2, on the facing page).

5 Using the side-profile template 'B', above, as a guide, cut and sand the angle at the base of the backrest. This area must be flat, or the base will not stick properly (see Fig 3 on the facing page).

Fig 1 Layouts for the seat base

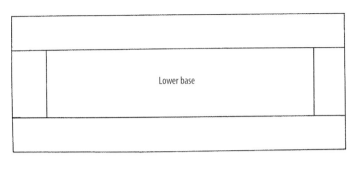

Lower base

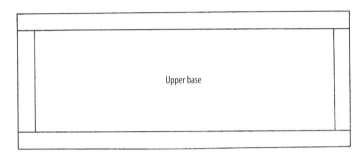

Upper base

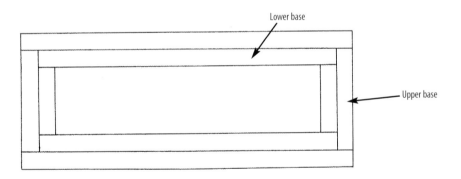

Lower base

Upper base

Fig 2 Backrest

Fig 3 Use the edge profile to mark the area to be removed

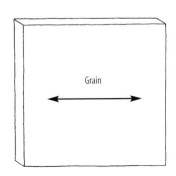

Grain

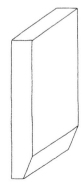

Fig 4 *Cut the dowel to the same width as the backrest*

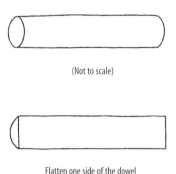

(Not to scale)

Flatten one side of the dowel

Fig 5 *Glue the dowel to the backrest*

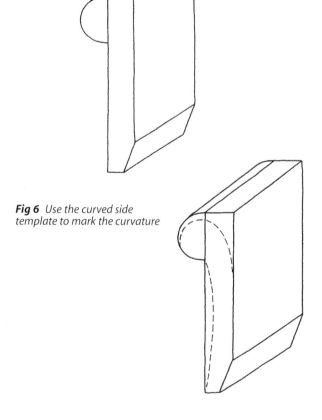

Fig 6 *Use the curved side template to mark the curvature*

Fig 7 *Shape the curvature with a craft knife, then sand until smooth*

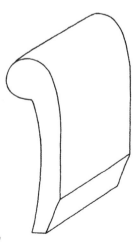

6 Cut a length of dowel the same width as the backrest cut in step 4, and flatten one side (Fig 4).

7 Glue to the top back edge of the backrest (Fig 5).

8 Use the curved, side template 'E', on page 82, to mark the curvature (see Fig 6, below left).

9 Use a craft knife and sandpaper to round off the top of the backrest until it forms a gentle curve into the dowel (see Fig 7, below).

10 Glue the sloping edge to the end of the seat base (see Fig 8, on facing page).

11 Drill 1/8in (3mm) into the tops of the cabriole legs, using a drill bit the same diameter as the cocktail sticks. Snip off the tapered end from the cocktail stick and discard. Dip the cut end into a little wood glue and insert into the drill hole in the top of the leg. Snip the cocktail stick to 1/4in (6mm) long. Continue until all of the legs are dowelled.

12 Use the same size drill bit on the underside of the seat base, to drill a hole 1/4in (6mm) in from each direction at all four corners. Glue the dowelled legs into the holes.

To finish, stain and polish, or paint the legs.

Fig 8 *Glue the sloping edge to the back of the seat assembly*

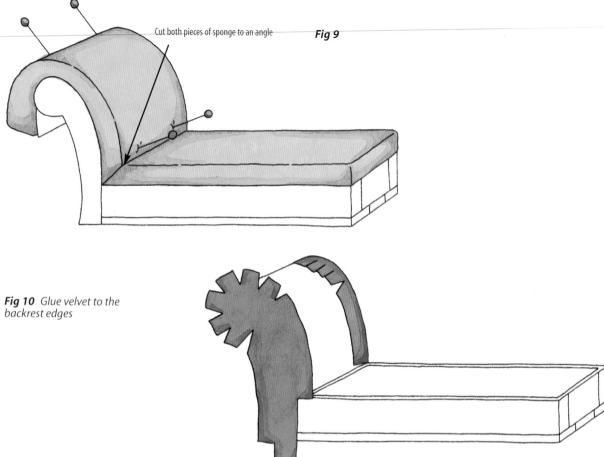

Cut both pieces of sponge to an angle

Fig 9

Fig 10 *Glue velvet to the backrest edges*

Upholstery

1 Cut a piece of the stiff lining fabric to fit the inside recess of the seat base, then glue the fabric in the seat well. Leave to dry, then fill the area with dry sand. Cut a second piece of the fabric to cover the whole surface of the seat. This top piece must not overhang the edges of the base, or it will show as a ridge when the upholstery fabric is in place. Glue on the top piece.

2 Check that the seat-base template 'A' will fit the top of the seat base and, if not, trim to fit. This card template now becomes the upholstery liner.

3 Cut a piece of foam the same size as the liner cut in step 2. Glue the foam to the card.

4 Cut a piece of thin card wide enough to fit the backrest exactly, and long enough to go right over the back roll and tuck just under the roll.

5 Cut a piece of foam the same width as the card liner prepared in step 4 and 1in (24mm) longer. Pin the card liner to the backrest and glue the foam to the card, removing and replacing the pins as you go. Set aside until the glue is dry.

6 At the backrest end of the liner/foam for the seat base (prepared in step 3), cut the foam to a 45° angle; this does not need to be precise, since the foam will squash down a little. Repeat with the bottom end of the backrest foam, where the two meet (see Fig 9, above). When the glue is dry remove from the chaise.

7 Cut two pieces of velvet large enough to cover the ends of the backrest with a 1/2in (12mm) overhang all around, and long enough to reach past the base of the seat at that point. Glue in position (see Fig 10, above).

Fig 11 *The velvet glued down over the curved edges*

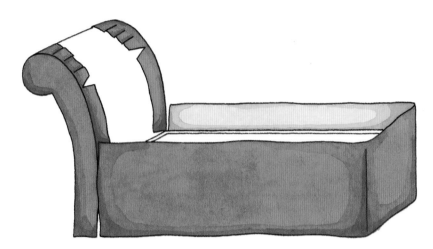

8 Snip into the corner under the backrest roll. Fold back and glue down the excess at both flat faces of the backrest. Spread glue over the reverse of the fabric at the curved area of the backrest. Pinch up the excess fabric into triangles as you stick the fabric down to the backrest. Make a tiny fold on the edge covering the base side.

9 Cut a 1¹/₂in (36mm) wide strip of velvet, long enough to stretch from the velvet applied to the base of the backrest on one side, right around the base to the same position on the other side.

Centre the strip on the base and glue in position. Spread glue on the reverse of the velvet overhang on the top surface. Fold the glued fabric over onto the seat and pinch the excess fabric into a triangle at each corner of the foot end of the seat. (See Fig 11, above, and Fig 12, below.)

10 Cut off the triangle at the corners, to give the impression of mitring. On the lower overhang, trim to fit neatly around the legs, spread glue on the reverse of the fabric and turn under the excess to the underside of the seat (see Fig 12, below).

Fig 12

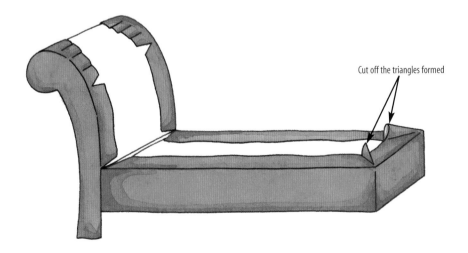

Cut off the triangles formed

11 Cut an 8¹⁄₂in (216mm) long strip of your chosen fabric for the centre panel. Cut a second piece of the fabric 5¹⁄₂in (140mm) long. For the contrasting side strips, cut two strips of velvet 8¹⁄₂in (216mm) long by 1¹⁄₂in (36mm) wide, and two strips of velvet 5¹⁄₂in (140mm) long by 1¹⁄₂in (36mm) wide. These pieces will be joined for the upholstery of the chaise longue (see step 12, below, and 'Note', below right).

12 If you are using a commercially made carpet runner, there will not be much spare fabric to use as a seam allowance. In this case, place the runner right sides together ¹⁄₄in (6mm) from the edge of the plain fabric and pin in position. Sew both fabrics together as close as possible to the edge of the runner. Put a small amount of glue between the fabrics on the seam allowance, press both fabrics together and trim off the excess plain fabric.

If you are printing the fabric yourself, the printed panel should be no wider than 1¹⁄₂in (3.8cm), but should have additional seam allowance on either side, for attaching the plain borders.

13 Sew one strip of velvet to either side of each piece of printed fabric of matching size, and then trim the seams back.

14 Centre the card and foam liner on the back of the seat cover, i.e. the longest piece (see Fig 13, below). Turn under the excess at both short ends and glue in position, do not stretch the fabric or in any way curve the card liner (Fig 14, opposite).

A note on cutting velvet

Be sure to cut the velvet so that all the nap, or pile, is facing in the same direction, otherwise it will appear to be two different shades. This can be effective when used intentionally as part of the design but is not desirable when it happens accidentally through a lack of care.

Fig 13 Centre the foam on the back of the sewn fabric

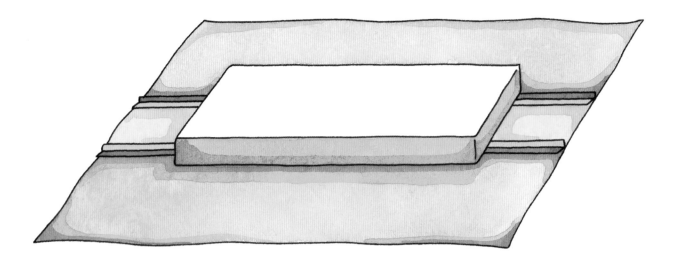

15 Tuck the excess fabric to the inside on all four corners and, with a matching thread, over-sew the corners to box the fabric (see Fig 14, right). Trim away the excess fabric from the inside to tidy up and lessen the bulkiness.

16 Turn under the excess at both long sides and glue to the card.

17 Spread glue over the seat base right up to the edges, being careful not to get any glue on the surface velvet. Pin the covered liner to the base and set aside until the glue is dry (Fig 15, right).

18 Next, cover the backrest liner: centre the previously joined 5¹/₂in (140mm) strips of fabric on the foam/card liner, turn under and glue the excess fabric at the base of the card (Fig 16, below).

Fig 14 *The short ends turned up and glued*

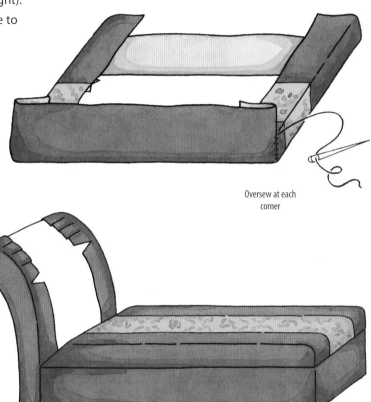

Oversew at each corner

Fig 15 *The covered liner in position*

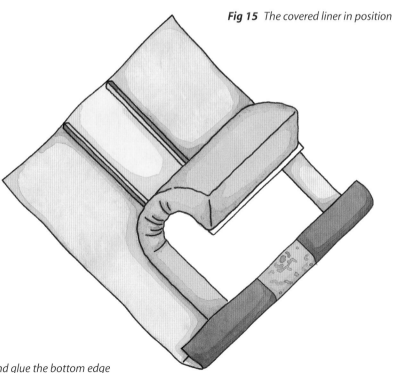

Fig 16 *Turn up and glue the bottom edge*

19 Turn under and glue the excess fabric to the card on both sides, evenly taking in the fullness around the curve (back roll position) as you go. Trim away the thickness formed on the underside of the back upholstery (see Fig 17, right).

20 Glue the covered liner to the backrest, then push firmly into the backrest corner. Pin in position until the glue is dry (see Fig 18, below right).

21 Pull back the fabric on the backrest to expose the card and foam, then trim the card and foam until it clears the join between the dowel and back. Straighten up the fabric again and trim until there is just enough to push into the join between the dowel and backrest. Be very careful not to trim off too much. It is easy to go back and trim off some more, but the whole back upholstery will be ruined if you take too much off initially. Run a line of glue into the join between the dowel and back and, using your flat, blunt tool, push the excess fabric into the join (see Fig 19, below).

Fig 17 Turn in and glue at the sides

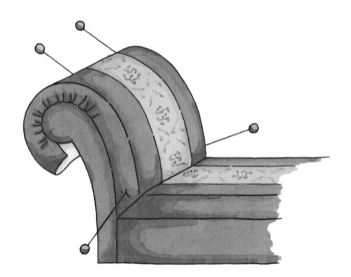

Fig 18 The backrest cover in position

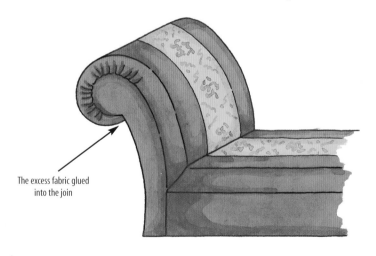

The excess fabric glued into the join

Fig 19

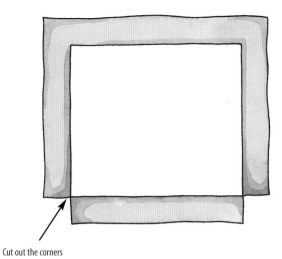

Cut out the corners

Fig 20 *Covering the back liner*

Fold over the fabric
and glue to the back of
the card

Fig 21

22 Cut a piece of card to fit from under the backrest roll to the base of the chaise longue. Cut a piece of plain velvet $\frac{1}{2}$in (12mm) larger all around than the card. Centre the card liner on the reverse of the velvet and glue in position (Fig 20, left).

23 Turn over the excess fabric on the top and two sides of the card liner, then glue to the back of the card, mitring the top corners. Cut off the excess fabric where it has folded over at the bottom corners (see Fig 21, below left).

24 Glue the covered back liner in position. Try to avoid glue oozing out at the sides but, if it does, wipe it off immediately with a barely damp cloth. Rub the edges with the flat edge of your blunt tool. Trim the bottom edge to fit neatly around the two back legs, then glue the excess fabric to the underside of the chaise longue (Fig 22, below).

Fig 22 *Gluing on the back liner*

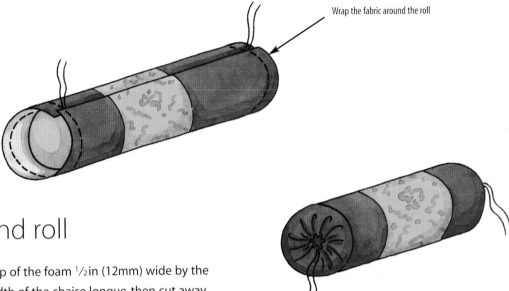

Fig 23 Sew a line of gathering stitches around the two edges of the fabric

Wrap the fabric around the roll

Fig 24 Draw up the gathers and fasten off the thread

The end roll

25 Cut a strip of the foam ¹/₂in (12mm) wide by the exact width of the chaise longue, then cut away the corners along the length of the foam until it is roughly spherical, rather like a short foam rod. Wrap a piece of wadding around the foam rod and slipstitch along the length of the rod shape to secure. The will increase the diameter of the foam to approximately ³/₈in (9mm).

26 Cut a piece of printed fabric, or carpet runner, for the centre panel, 3¹/₂in (86mm) long and no more than 1¹/₂in (38mm) wide. Cut two strips of velvet 3¹/₂in (86mm) long and ³/₄in (18mm) wide. Sew one strip of velvet to each side of the printed fabric. Trim seams.

27 Wrap the fabric around the foam roll and overlap the edges (Fig 23, above). Over-sew the raw edge to the roll (it will be hidden when the roll is attached).

28 Check that the plain velvet at each side is just long enough to reach the centre when it is turned over the ends of the roll. If it is too long, then trim.

29 Sew a line of small running stitches (gathers) around the edges of the plain velvet on both ends of the roll. Before pulling up the gathers, put a little glue on the end of your finger and wipe it onto the reverse of the velvet. Pull up the gathers and fasten off (Fig 24).

30 To complete the roll, spread glue on the underside where it was stitched closed. Position at the foot of the chaise and pin in place until the glue is dry.

31 Cut a piece of the stiff fabric to fit the underside of the chaise seat. Trim to fit around the insides of the legs and to cover half of the velvet glued to the underside of the chaise. Glue in position.

The cushions

32 Make a small cushion, 1¹/₂ x 1¹/₄in (36 x 30mm), using the printed fabric or carpet runner (see instructions for making cushions on page 9). Half-fill the cushion with dry sand.

33 Make a larger cushion, 1³/₄in (44mm) square, using the plain velvet. Half-fill this one with dry sand, too.

The final trimming

Trim the chaise with tassels and fringes. I cut down and adapted a full-size trim – there is no hard-and-fast rule about the size of trims used on furniture. Our ancestors used a huge variety of different sizes and shapes, many more than we have today. Sometimes just removing a couple of rows of stitching and cutting shorter will give a very acceptable rich look, so if it looks right and you are happy, that is all that matters.

This particular chaise is meant to look ornate and sumptuous and definitely over the top. A few tiny tassels in gold attached to the corners of the cushions, or even attached to a cord and swagged along the fringing would not look out of place.

Tip
To remove stitch marks and creases from a trimming, hold it over a steaming pan or kettle.

Buttoned Chaise Longue in Black Leather

The only difference in the wooden structure for this chaise and the Velvet-covered Chaise is that I have added a slope to the back, for which you will need a 1in (24mm) square of balsa wood. I have also used different legs (although cabriole legs would look just as good) and black leather to cover the chaise longue.

The wooden structure

Fig 1 *Make a diagonal cut across the square of balsa*

Fig 2 *It may be necessary to adjust the back edge with sandpaper, so that it fits the angle of the backrest*

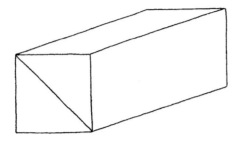

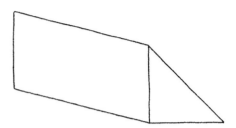

To construct this chaise longue

1 For the wooden framework, follow steps 1–10 for the velvet-covered chaise longue (see pages 82–4).

2 Next, cut a piece of 1in (24mm) square balsa wood to the exact width of the chaise. If you do not have balsa wood in this size, glue together smaller strips until you have the correct dimensions, and then treat the block as one piece.

3 Cut diagonally across the square of balsa, to make two triangular pieces (Figs 1 and 2, above).

4 Discard one of the triangular pieces and glue the remaining one into the join between the backrest and the seat (see Fig 3, below). The back edge of the wedge may need a little adjustment to fit the angle of the backrest. Allow the glue to dry before proceeding.

5 Take a piece of scrap dowel, wrap sandpaper around it and use this to sand the triangular wedge to a nice curved shape (see Fig 4, opposite).

Fig 3 *Glue the wedge into the angle between the backrest and the seat*

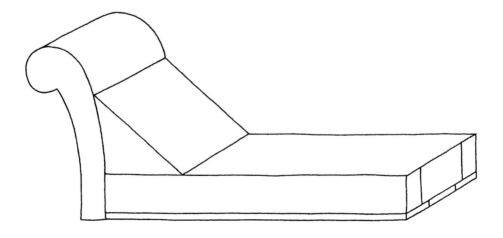

Fig 4 Sand the wedge to a curve

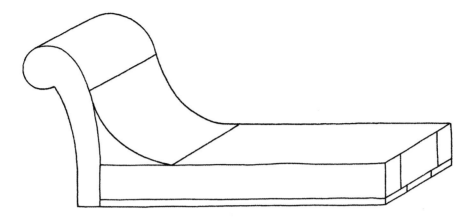

Fig 5 Cover all side edges with thin card

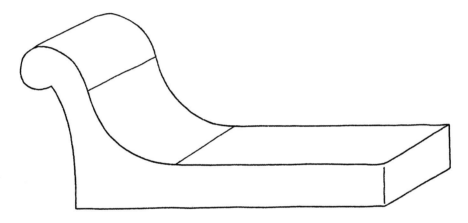

Upholstery

6 Make sure the wood on the sides is completely smooth and level, as any imperfection will show beneath fine leather, including deep wood grain and joins in the wood. Glue card over all of the wood on both sides of the chaise, to hide the joins. Try to apply the card in one piece, as this will prevent any wood or card joins from showing through the leather.

The chaise is now ready for upholstery. The whole surface of the chaise is upholstered in one piece.

Follow step 1 under 'Upholstery' in the previous chaise instructions for applying the layer of stiff fabric to the seat (see page 86).

1 To prepare the liner, photocopy or trace the template overleaf onto thin card, taking care to transfer all the markings. I have drawn the liner a little longer than required, to take into account variations in making up the chaise longue, but the length can be adjusted during the upholstery process. Make sure that the liner is the exact width

Template for the liner, showing positions for 'buttoning'

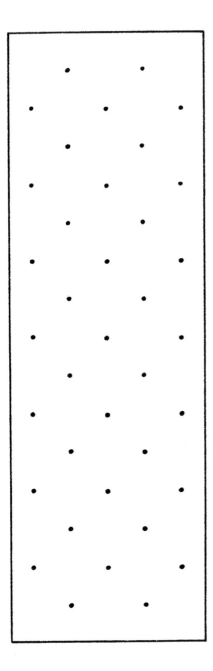

of your chaise with no overhang of card. If you need to trim the card, then take an equal amount off both long sides, to keep the buttoning pattern correct and central. The two outer rows of dots can be omitted if, after trimming, they are too close to the edge.

2 Cut a piece of foam to the exact width of the card liner and 2in (48mm) longer at the backrest end.

3 Curve the liner to the shape of the chaise seat surface and pin in position around the backrest roll, making sure that the markings are on the underside of the card. Glue the foam to the card and tape in position at intervals along its length, removing and replacing the pins through the foam around the backrest. Allow the glue to dry before proceeding, so that the card/foam sets into the curved shape.

4 Remove the foam/liner from the chaise and set aside. Cover the seat base and backrest sides with leather, following the instructions for steps 7–9 for the previous chaise longue (see pages 86–7), but substituting leather for velvet. Include the wedge shape, and cover in one piece, if possible.

5 Cut a piece of leather 2in (48mm) larger on all sides than the foam/card liner. Centre the foam side over the reverse of the leather.

6 Using a needle for sewing leather, and doubled thread to match the leather, begin to 'button' the leather at the foot end. To do this, start with the needle at the back and take it through the card, through the foam and leather and out to the front. Re-insert the needle a short distance from its exit point, not more than $1/16$in (1.5mm) away, and take it through to the back. Pull the thread to indent the leather and tie the thread to the end hanging from the back, do not cut the thread. Insert the needle into the next mark on the card and repeat, but when the thread is returned to the back this time, use the needle to work a knot on the thread bridging the marks (see Fig 6, facing page). Repeat at each mark.

Fig 6 *The stitching pattern*

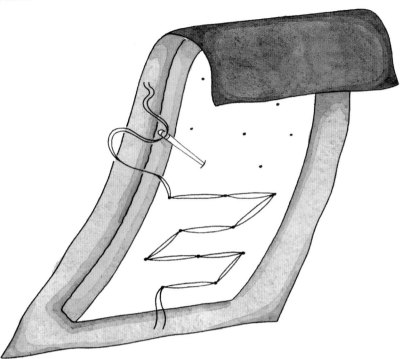

7 Turn under the excess leather at the foot end of the upholstery, and glue to the back of the card. Do not pull too tightly or the card will curve and the upholstery will no longer fit.

8 Before folding under and gluing the sides, deal with the foot-end corners: spread glue around each corner on the inside surface of the leather and, on the face of the leather, pinch the corner edges very tightly with a pair of flat-bladed pliers (see Fig 7, right). Leave until the glue is completely dry.

Fig 7

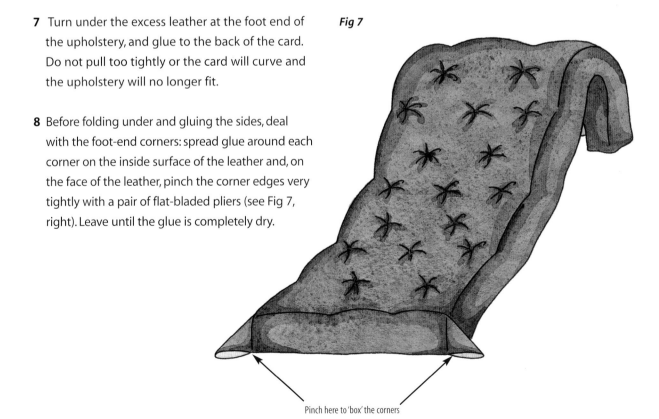

Pinch here to 'box' the corners

9 When the glue is dry, trim each corner as closely as you can without opening the seams. If you inadvertently open one, then use your flat-bladed tool to spread a little glue on the inside of the seam and then pinch again with pliers.

10 Turn under the leather and glue it to the card liner on each long side, mitring the corners at the foot end on the underside. As you do this, ease in the fullness on the curves at the backrest end of the upholstery. Trim off any triangles formed.

11 Spread glue on the seat and backrest surface, making sure that the glue goes right up to the edges. Position the covered pad over the glued area, lining up the foot and side edges. If any glue oozes out, wipe it off immediately with a damp sponge. Press the side joins firmly to get good adhesion. Cover the leather surfaces with a cloth or paper to protect the leather and use masking tape wrapped around the upholstery to hold the seat in position while the glue dries.

12 Finish the backrest roll and the back liner as in steps 18 to 24 for the Velvet-covered Chaise (see pages 89–91). Cover the underside with a piece of stiff fabric trimmed to fit around the legs.

Polish the leather with a little shoe cream or, as in my example, with a little black boot polish, and your chaise is complete.

Blue Leather Chaise Longue

The only difference between the structure of this chaise and the first one is the addition of a side rail. The upholstery is plainer, and I am reliably informed that a chaise in this colour is usually only found in a doctor's surgery.

Materials and Equipment

For the side rail:

3in (72mm) length of $^3/_{16}$ in (4.5mm) square pine or jelutong

3in (72mm) length of $^3/_{16}$ x $^1/_{16}$ in (4.5 x 1.5mm) pine or jelutong strip

3$^1/_4$ in (78mm) length of $^3/_{16}$ x $^1/_{16}$ in (4.5 x 1.5mm) pine or jelutong strip

For the legs:

2 strips of tiny turnings. These strips can be purchased in several styles, usually with three sizes of turnings, small, medium and large. I have used the medium size for this project.

To make the side rail

1 Cut eight small turnings with a dowel at each end (this is why you will need two strips).

2 Tape together the 3 x $^3/_{16}$ in (72 x 4.5mm) square wood strip and the 3 x $^3/_{16}$ x $^1/_{16}$ in (72 x 4.5 x 1.5mm) strip. Mark for drilling at $^3/_8$ in (9mm) intervals along the top surface of the thinner strip (see Fig 1, below).

3 At each marked position drill a hole $^1/_4$ in (6mm) deep. The drilled hole will penetrate right through the thinner strip and $^1/_{16}$ in (1.5mm) into the thicker section. Use a drill bit the same size as the dowels on each end of the tiny turned parts. It will help to

wind a small piece of masking tape around the drill bit $^1/_4$ in from the end and then drill only up to the edge of the tape. Make sure that the dowels at each end of the turned parts are no longer than $^1/_{16}$ in (1.5mm).

4 Remove the masking tape from the strips, then stain the strips and the turned spindles.

5 Dip the dowel end of each spindle into a little wood glue and insert one in each drill hole in the $^3/_{16}$ in (4.5mm) square strip.

6 Put a spot of glue on the other dowel end of each spindle and position the thinner strip so that each dowel goes into the corresponding hole (Fig 2, below).

Fig 1 *Strips joined with tape and marked for drilling*

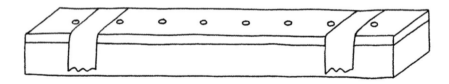

Fig 2 *Assembling the rail*

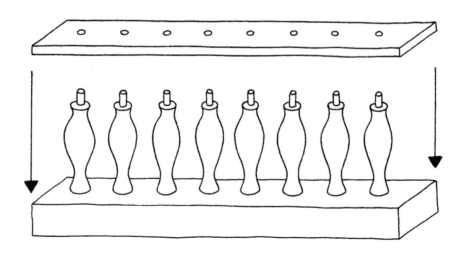

Fig 3 *Glue on the top strip*

Round off the front edge

7 Glue on the undrilled 3¼in (78mm) long top strip, so that it overlaps at the back by ⅛in (3mm), then round off the front edge (as shown in Fig 3, above).

8 Try-fit the rail assembly on the chaise and mark the position of the top overlapping rail strip.

9 Cut a slot ¹⁄₁₆in (1.5mm) high, ⅛in (3mm) deep and ⅛in (3mm) wide, as marked in step 8 (see Fig 4, below).

10 Glue the side rail in position. The base of the rail will stick out ¹⁄₁₆in (1.5mm) from the base, to allow for the upholstery thickness.

11 Varnish or polish the rail and legs as desired.

Fig 4

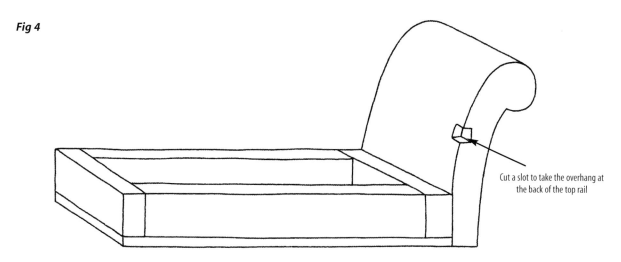

Cut a slot to take the overhang at the back of the top rail

The completed framework

Upholstery

The upholstery for this chaise is the same as given for the velvet chaise longue on page 86, apart from the following exceptions:

- The card liner for the seat is trimmed to fit inside the back rail.

- The backrest side-covering is trimmed to fit around the rail where it is joined to the backrest.

- The leather covering the seat-foam must be long enough to cover the base sides at the front and foot edges.

- On the side with the rail, the leather is folded under the card at the recessed area, and the rest covers the side of the seat base.

- A short length of leather is cut to fit under the side rail on the seat base.

On this example I have also made a roll cushion and finished it with a leather tassel on each end. The tassels are from narrow strips of leather. Instructions for making the cushion are given in the first chaise instructions on page 92.

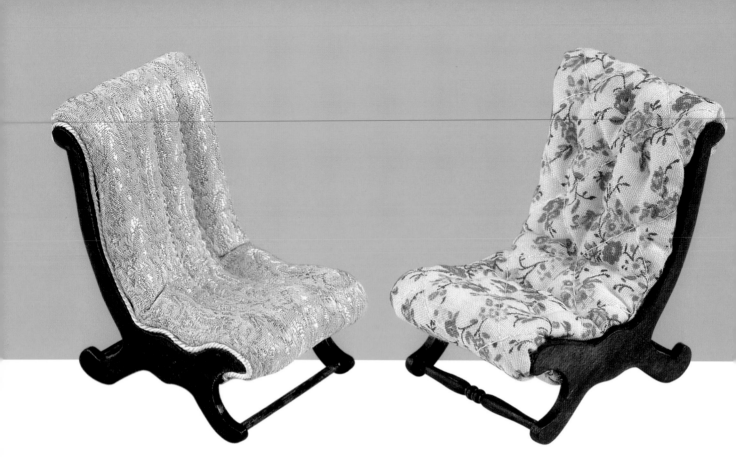

Slipper Chair

This Victorian chair, which is very simple to construct, has often been described erroneously as a nursing chair. It would indeed offer a very comfortable position for nursing a child and I have no doubt that it would have been used for that purpose in later years. However, very few upper-class Victorian ladies fed, or looked after, their own children – that was what the wet nurse and nanny were for – and the furniture they used was very definitely utilitarian.

Materials and Equipment

1/16 in (1.5mm) sheet hardwood, preferably jelutong

3/32 in (2.25mm) sheet hardwood, preferably jelutong

3/16 in (4.5mm) dowel

1/16 in (1.5mm) dowel, or cocktail stick

Wood glue

Water soluble gum

Thin card

Wood stain

Varnish, as preferred

A small piece of firm, lining fabric (see page 7)

1/4 in (6mm) foam

1/16 in (1.5mm) drill bit in a pin vice or mini drill (see 'Tip', right)

Fabric of your choice (I have used cream silk)

Trimming, if desired

Templates for the wooden framework

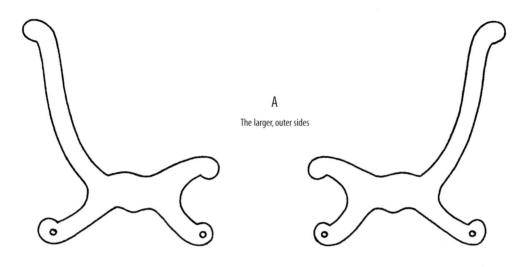

A

The larger, outer sides

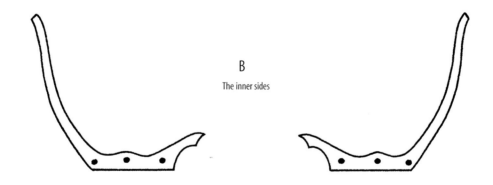

B

The inner sides

<table>
<tr><td>

Tip

A pin vice is preferable to a mini drill, as it offers more control over the depth of penetration when drilling such small pieces. You can tell the size of a drill bit by measuring the untwisted end across its diameter.

</td></tr>
</table>

Traditionally the slipper chair was found in the bedroom or morning room, and it would look very effective in either of these rooms. It is a very feminine and comfortable chair, which would never have been found in a Victorian nursery, as it was too good for servant use.

Two examples are shown on page 106, to show a different treatment of fabric: a floral, diamond-quilted example and a cream silk, lengthwise-quilted example. The only difference between the two versions is the quilting, and here I give instructions for the cream silk version.

Constructing the framework

Trace or photocopy templates 'A' and 'B' (on the previous page) onto ordinary paper, not card as with the earlier templates. Make one set of each, as shown, so that each diagram has a mirror image, and cut out.

Note

The glued-on paper strengthens the wood until it is stabilized by the construction, a method commonly used in veneer work where there are many small parts which are liable to break.

Water-soluble gum must be used, as the paper will need to be removed at a later stage.

1   Pre-stain a piece of the $^3/_{32}$ in (2.25mm) hardwood that is sufficiently large to take template 'A', the larger outer sides. Allow the stain to dry completely, then use water-soluble gum to stick both paper templates 'A' to the stained surface (see Fig 1, below).

2   Repeat step 1 with template 'B' (the inner sides) but do not stain the wood and, this time, use $^1/_{16}$ in (1.5mm) hardwood. Cut out the shapes, using a hand or electric fretsaw (see Fig 2, on facing page).

Fig 1 *Templates 'A' glued onto $^3/_{32}$in (2.25mm) hardwood*

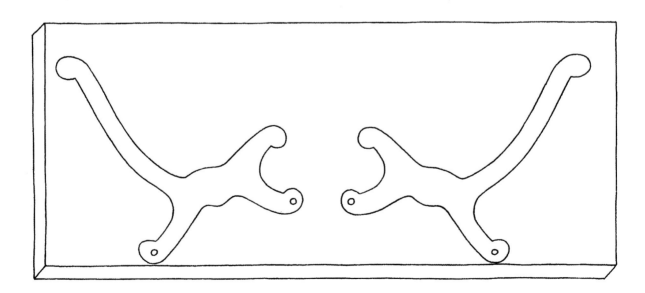

Fig 2 Templates 'B' glued to $^1/_{16}$in (1.5mm) hardwood

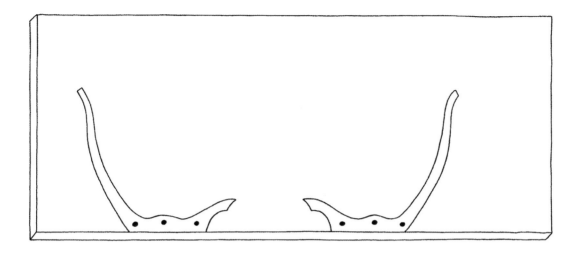

3 Place the larger, outer sides 'A' together, with the edges aligned. Hold firmly together and, with a piece of sandpaper wrapped around a pencil, smooth and level the edges of both pieces, as a single unit, to make both parts identical. Repeat the procedure with the smaller inner 'B' sides.

4 Drill $^1/_{16}$in (1.5mm) holes into the smaller set of sides at the positions marked on the paper template. This is best done while the sides are held down on a flat surface – the holes can go right through the wood.

5 Glue the smaller inner 'B' sides to the inside of the larger 'A' sides, with the bare wood sides together. Do not glue to the paper side, as it would then be impossible to remove the paper. The inner sides must be positioned in precisely the same position on each outer sides, and also recessed $^1/_{16}$in (1.5mm) from the top edge (see Fig 3, below).

Fig 3 Gluing the inner sides to the outer sides

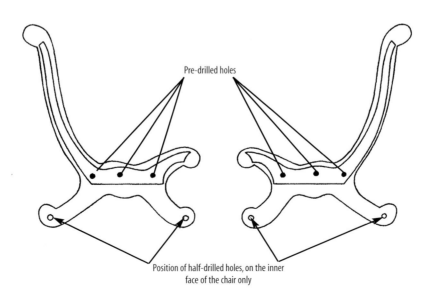

Pre-drilled holes

Position of half-drilled holes, on the inner
face of the chair only

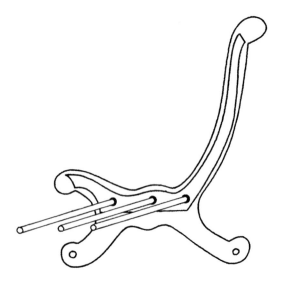

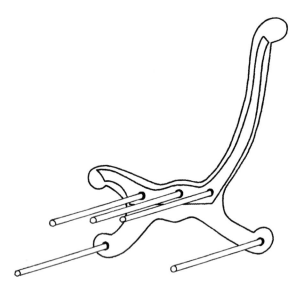

Fig 4 *Inserting the seat dowels*

Fig 5 *Inserting the stretcher dowels*

6 Cut two lengths of ³/₁₆in (4.5mm) dowel 1³/₈in (35mm) long.

7 Cut three lengths of ¹/₁₆in (1.5mm) dowel (or cocktail sticks) also 1³/₈in (35mm) long.

8 Cut two lengths of ¹/₁₆in (1.5mm) dowel (or cocktail stick) 1⁷/₁₆in (36.5mm) long.

9 Measure ¹/₃₂in (0.75mm) from the twisted end of the drill bit and wrap a small piece of masking tape at this point. This will determine the depth of the last set of holes.

10 Mark the position for the set of drill holes on the inner part of the larger chair sides.

11 Drill the hole as marked, to the depth of the masking tape. DO NOT drill all the way through the wood, as the outer face of the chair must remain smooth.

12 Stain the edges and inner sides of the outer frame before any gluing takes place, as the stain will not penetrate through glue. Then, dip the end of each of the three ¹/₁₆ x 1³/₈in (1.5 x 35mm) seat dowels into a little wood glue before inserting them into the drill holes on one of the chair sides (see Fig 4, above left). Immediately wipe off any excess glue with a damp sponge.

13 Insert the two ¹/₁₆ x 1⁷/₈in (1.5 x 36.5mm) stretcher dowels into the bottom holes on the same sidepiece (see Fig 5, left).

14 Put a dot of wood glue onto the exposed ends of the dowels and insert them into the corresponding drill holes on the second side (Fig 6, facing page).

15 Stand the chair upright on a level surface, check that it is not twisted in any way, then leave alone until the glue is completely hard, about 24 hours.

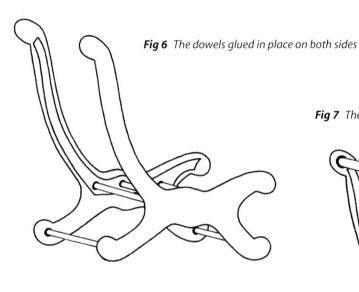

Fig 6 *The dowels glued in place on both sides*

Fig 7 *The top and seat front rolls in place*

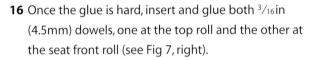

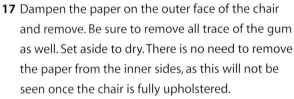

16 Once the glue is hard, insert and glue both $^3/_{16}$ in (4.5mm) dowels, one at the top roll and the other at the seat front roll (see Fig 7, right).

17 Dampen the paper on the outer face of the chair and remove. Be sure to remove all trace of the gum as well. Set aside to dry. There is no need to remove the paper from the inner sides, as this will not be seen once the chair is fully upholstered.

18 Varnish as preferred.

The completed framework

Upholstery

The upholstery of this chair is as simple as its construction.

1 Cut a piece of the firm lining fabric, wide enough to fit between the outer sides, and long enough to curve around the front roll. Curve it gently over the inner frame of the seat and over the top roll.

2 Cut a piece of foam the exact width of the lining fabric and 1/2 in (12mm) longer at both ends.

3 Cut a piece of your chosen upholstery fabric for the top cover, 1in (24mm) larger all around than the foam cut in the previous step.

4 Lay the upholstery fabric face down on a flat surface, place the foam centrally over it, and the firm fabric centrally on top of the foam. Tack through all layers very loosely.

5 Either machine or hand sew down the centre length through all three layers. If you are sewing by hand, use a backstitch and pull each stitch tight to obtain the ridged effect.

6 Sew a second row 1/2 in (12mm) from the first, and a third on the opposite side of the initial row. You will end up with three parallel rows running the length of the sandwich (see Fig 8, below).

7 Fold over the excess printed fabric on each long edge and glue to the backing fabric. Do not overstretch the fabric while doing this. Try-fit the upholstery on the chair to make sure that it will fit between the sides without exposing any of the underlying woodwork.

8 Run a line of PVA glue along the recessed inner sides. Centre the upholstery pad on the recess, then pin through the upholstery to the frame below to hold the padding in position.

Fig 8 *The three parallel rows of stitching*

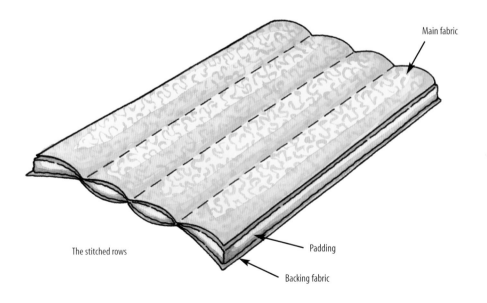

Main fabric

The stitched rows

Padding

Backing fabric

Fig 9 *Stitching around the crossbar*

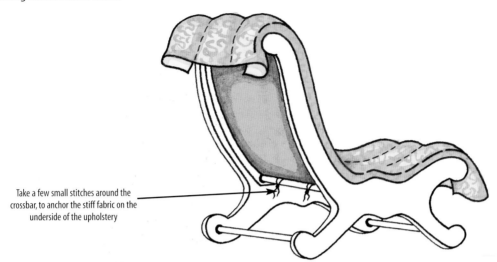

Take a few small stitches around the
crossbar, to anchor the stiff fabric on the
underside of the upholstery

9 On the underside take a few small stitches around
the dowel crossbars and into the backing fabric. This
will anchor the upholstery in place (see Fig 9, above).

10 Try-fit the upholstery sandwich around the
front rail. If you need to reduce the length, fold
back the top fabric and trim the foam first. You
may need to unpick some of the stitches used to
quilt the fabric. Make sure that you only trim the
necessary amount, and that you leave enough to
curve right around the seat front rail to the
underside, without forcing or stretching the
fabrics. Straighten up the fabric cover and glue
or sew to the underside (see Fig 10, right).

11 Cut a piece of thin card wide enough to fit
between the chair sides and long enough to fit
between the underside of the top roll and the
underside of the chair front roll.

12 Cover the card with the upholstery fabric used for
the seat-top covering. Turn under any raw edges
and glue to the back of the card, removing any
excess thickness as you do this.

Fig 10 *The fabric around the top and front rails*

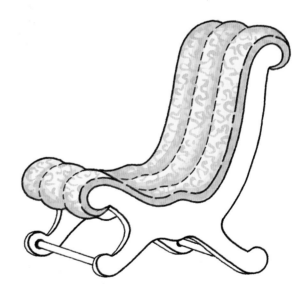

13 Glue the backing in position and sew with small stitches and matching thread to the underside of both top and front rolls (see Fig 11, right).

14 Trim with braids and cords, if you wish, and your chair is then complete.

Fig 11 *The backing in position*

Victorian Bedroom Chair

This dainty little chair was found in many Victorian bedrooms. Like the slipper chair, it was often, incorrectly, called a nursing chair. Before the twentieth century people used their bedroom for much more than sleeping and it was probably the most private place the upper classes had to escape to during the Victorian era. In previous centuries the bedroom was even used for entertaining and, during the seventeenth century, aristocratic ladies would invite a select group of favourites to attend their toilette, both male and female.

Materials and Equipment (see page 121, also)

Thin card for templates	Cocktail stick for use as dowels
$3/16$ in (4.5mm) dowel	Wood glue
$3/16$ in (4.5mm) jelutong or any other hardwood sheet	Wood finishing materials
$1/4$ x $1/8$ in (6 x 3mm) stripwood (any wood, except balsa)	Foam $1/4$ in (6mm) thick
2 pre-made legs $11/16$ in (18mm) high	Fabric for upholstery

Templates for the wooden framework

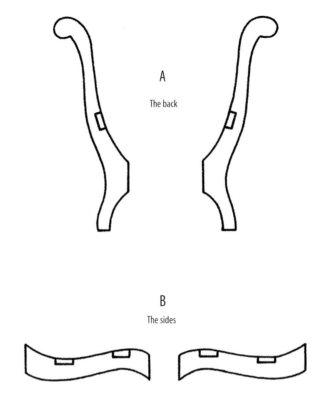

A

The back

B

The sides

Fig 1 *Layout for the back and side templates (not to scale)*

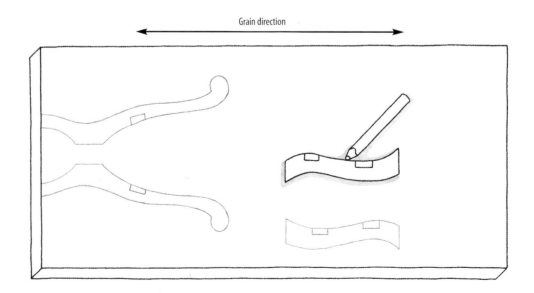

Grain direction

Construction

This chair is easy to construct, as it has very few parts and uses bought legs. If you have difficulty finding suitable legs, then it is possible to adapt a pair of staircase spindles, but use only the chunky type with a square top.

1 Prepare templates 'A' and 'B', on the facing page, by photocopying, tracing or scanning the shapes onto thin card, then cut them out accurately.

2 Lay the back and sides shapes 'A' and 'B' on $^3/_{16}$in (4.5mm) hardwood sheet, making sure that the grain direction is as shown in the diagram of the layout (Fig 1 on the facing page). Draw around the shapes, then cut out using a hand or electric fretsaw.

3 Cut one piece of $^3/_{16}$in (4.5mm) dowel, $1^1/_{16}$in (25.5mm) long, for the top stretcher roll.

4 From $^1/_4$ x $^1/_8$in (6 x 3mm) stripwood cut three pieces $1^1/_4$in (30mm) long. From the same wood cut one piece $1^1/_2$in (36mm) long, and another piece 1in (24mm) long. These are for the front rails.

5 Now for the only tricky bit, which is cutting one rebate on each back part. I usually do this, very carefully, with a sharp craft knife. The rebate needs to be $^1/_4$in (6mm) long x $^1/_{16}$in (1.5mm) wide x $^1/_{16}$in (1.5mm) deep. Remember that all woodwork on the inside structure of the chair will be hidden, so it does not need to be perfect, just make sure that the rebate is in the same position on both side parts. (See Fig 2, bottom left, for reference and the 'Note' below.)

6 Cut the rebates on both side parts, referring to Fig 3 (below right) for the position. The rebates should be exactly the same size as the ones on the back parts.

Note

Because of the shape of the back parts, you cannot lay them on their back on a flat surface to cut the rebates, and the pieces will snap if you attempt to cut the rebates without support. To overcome this, make a firm pad of folded waste fabric and tuck it under the back part to support the area you are working on. Make sure that the rebates are cut only on the inside face of the back, as they should not be visible on the outer surface.

Fig 2 *Cutting the back rebate*

Fig 3 *Cutting the side rebates*

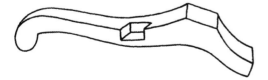

7 Using a ¹⁄₁₆in (1.5mm) drill bit, drill a hole ¹⁄₈in (3mm) deep on the back parts at the position marked in Fig 4, right. Wrap a small piece of masking tape around the drill bit ¹⁄₈in (3mm) from the end and drill only to this depth.

8 On the side parts find the centre of each end and drill a hole ¹⁄₈in (3mm) deep (see Fig 5, below).

Fig 4 *Cutting the back rebate*

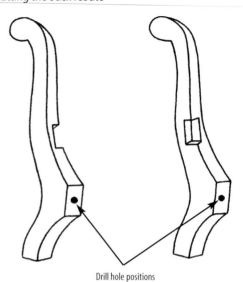

Drill hole positions

Fig 5 *The rebates on the side parts and position of the drill holes*

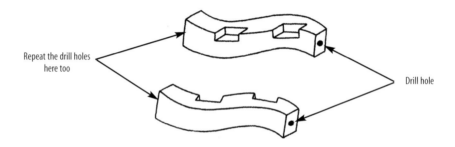

Repeat the drill holes here too

Drill hole

Fig 6 *Glue a leg to each end of the wood strip*

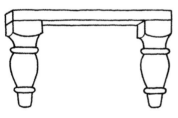

Fig 7 *Glue the shorter strip of wood between the legs*

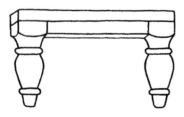

9 Glue one leg to each end of the 1¹⁄₂in (36mm) long piece of stripwood cut in step 4 (page 117), as shown in Fig 6, left.

10 Glue the 1in (24mm) piece of stripwood between the legs, i.e. underneath the strip attached in step nine (see Fig 7, left). Set aside until the glue is completely dry.

11 Cut the tapered end from a cocktail stick and discard. Dab a little wood glue onto the end of the remaining piece and insert the end into the hole drilled into the back parts. Cut the remaining cocktail stick down to ¹⁄₈in (3mm). Repeat on the second back piece.

Fig 8 The side glued onto the dowel in the back

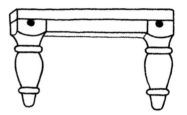

Fig 9 The drill hole position on the back of the top of the legs

12 Put a little spot of glue on the dowel in the back and firmly insert it into the hole drilled into the back of the side part (see Fig 8, above). Repeat on the second back and side part.

Fig 10 The leg assembly glued onto the dowelled fronts of the side parts

13 Drill a ¹/₁₆in (3mm) hole just below centre on the back top of each leg (see Fig 9, above right).

14 Dowel the legs in the same manner as the back. Glue the dowels and insert them into the holes drilled into the front of the side parts (Fig 10, right).

15 Using the three strips from step 4 (page 117), cut a rebate ¹/₁₆in (1.5mm) deep, ¹/₁₆in (1.5mm) wide on each end of all three pieces (see Fig 11, below).

Fig 11 Cutting the rebates on the spars

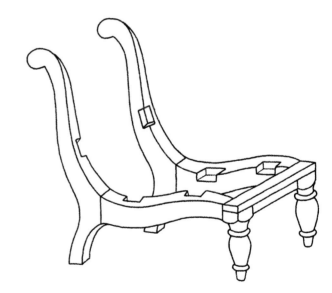

The front sanded to match the seat curvature

Fig 12 *Inserting the spars into the rebates in the side assembly*   **Fig 13** *Top roll in position*

16 Glue the support spars into the rebates cut into the body of the chair (see Fig 12, above).

17 Glue in the roll, cut in step 3 (page 117), at the top between the back side parts (see Fig 13, top right). Leave the chair for at least 24 hours, to dry.

18 Round off the front edge until it forms a gentle curve on the seat front, referring to Fig 13 (above) and the pictures of the finished chair structure, below.

19 Stain and varnish the sides, back and legs.

The completed framework

Upholstery

This chair is upholstered in a very similar way to the slipper chair (see pages 112–14), except that it has no lengthwise quilting. However, if you use a plush fabric like velvet, a little bit of quilting would add a hint of luxury.

1 Cut a piece of stiff fabric long enough to curve over the seat front 1/8in (3mm) above the legs, curve gently over the inner frame of the seat and back, and over the back top roll. The fabric needs to fit between the chair sides (see Fig 14, below). Glue in position.

2 Cut a piece of thin card to fit from the front rail just above the legs to the top roll, curving gently over the seat. It must fit the whole width of the chair from outside edge to outside edge. (Omit this step if you intend to quilt the fabric; instead cut a second piece of stiff fabric to the same size as the card, but this must be the exact width of the chair.)

> **To upholster this chair you will need:**
>
> Fabric of your choice
> Sewing needle and matching thread
> Tacky glue
> Small piece of stiff fabric 4in (100mm) square (see page 7)
> Small piece of thin card 4in (100mm) square
> Small piece of 1/4in (6mm) foam, also 4in (100mm) square
> Low tack masking tape (to make masking tape low tack apply it to a piece of fabric and rip it of a few times)

3 Cut a piece of foam to the same width as the card or fabric and 1in (24mm) longer at each end.

Fig 14 *The stiff fabric in position*

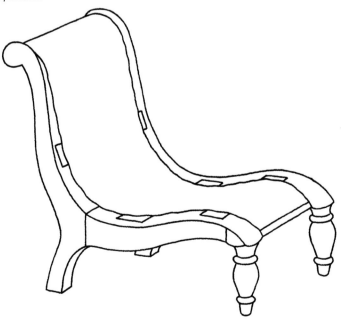

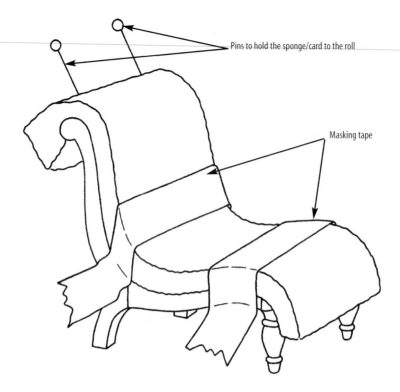

Pins to hold the sponge/card to the roll

Masking tape

Fig 15 *The sponge being glued to the card*

4 Curve the card to the shape of the chair. Glue the foam to the card, ensuring that you have 1in (24mm) of foam protruding at both ends. Lightly tape to the chair until the glue is dry (see Fig 15, above).

5 If you intend to quilt the fabric, omit step 4 and follow steps 1–6 for the slipper chair on page 112.

6 Cut a piece of fabric ¼in (6mm) larger all around than the foam/card liner – the excess ¼in (6mm) is a seam allowance.

7 Cut two strips of fabric ³⁄₄in (18mm) wide and the same length as the main piece cut in step 6.

8 Take the main piece of fabric and one of the narrow pieces; place them right sides together, matching the edges, and sew a ¼in (6mm) seam, using a small backstitch or a small machine stitch. Repeat on the opposite side. Trim the seam back to ¹⁄₈in (3mm) and press towards the centre. (This is important to the final finish of the chair.)

9 Remove the foam/card from the chair. Centre the fabric over the foam and carefully smooth it to the curvature of the foam. Glue the excess fabric from the side strips to the back of the card liner at the sides. Do not pull the fabric too tight or you will distort the seams, and do not glue the fabric to the foam.

If you want the fabric to be particularly smooth, you can cover the foam with lengths of lightweight double-sided sticky tape, which will grip the top fabric. However, if you intend doing this, then be aware that I have never found a tape yet that will not degrade and turn brittle. Also, you must ensure that the foam/card liner is exactly the same curvature as the chair or the fabric/foam/card sandwich will crease when fitted and ruin the whole effect.

10 Fold back the fabric at both ends and trim the foam to fit just above the front legs and under the top roll.

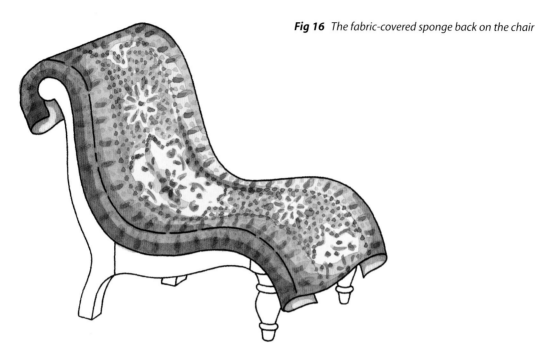

Fig 16 *The fabric-covered sponge back on the chair*

11 Run a line of glue along each side of the chair, close to the edge, and spread some on the stiff fabric covering the framework. Position the fabric-covered foam on the chair. Hold in position with low-tack masking tape until the glue is dry (see Fig 16, above – masking tape omitted for clarity).

12 Run a line of glue along the front rail just above the legs and glue down the fabric. Trim around the front of the legs and glue the excess between the legs, to the underside of the chair (Fig 17, right). It may be necessary to trim the fabric a little, before turning it under the chair, to reduce the bulk.

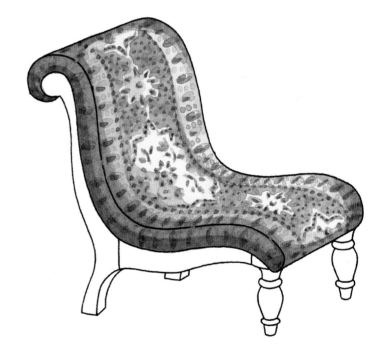

Fig 17 *Fabric and sponge trimmed and remaining fabric glued in place*

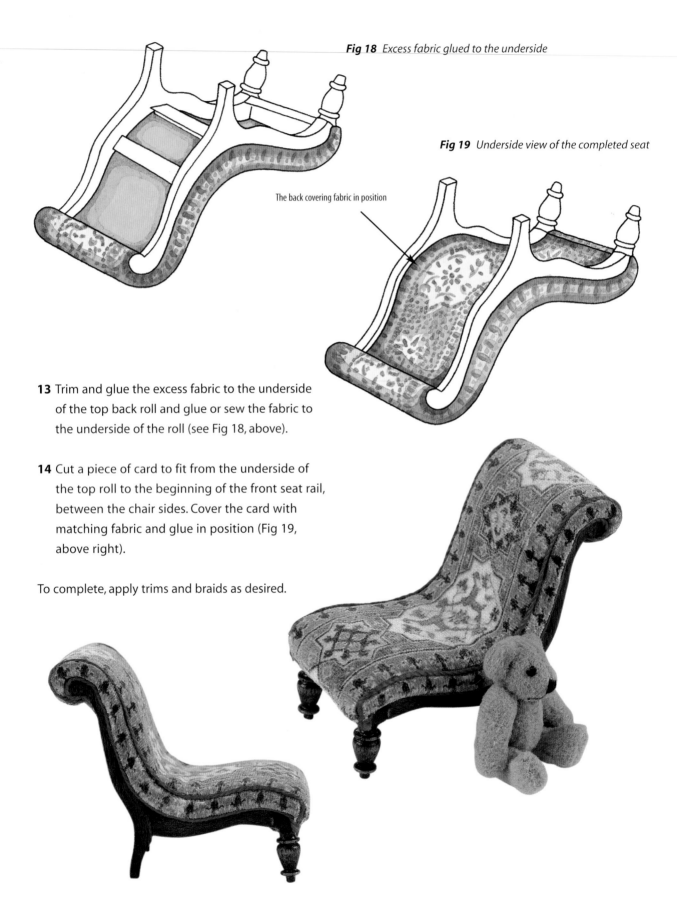

Fig 18 *Excess fabric glued to the underside*

Fig 19 *Underside view of the completed seat*

The back covering fabric in position

13 Trim and glue the excess fabric to the underside of the top back roll and glue or sew the fabric to the underside of the roll (see Fig 18, above).

14 Cut a piece of card to fit from the underside of the top roll to the beginning of the front seat rail, between the chair sides. Cover the card with matching fabric and glue in position (Fig 19, above right).

To complete, apply trims and braids as desired.

Heavy Victorian Parlour chair

This chair is constructed very simply. As with the bolster-back chair, I have made two versions: the one in sculptured devoré velvet (above right) is constructed authentically, while the one upholstered in Florentine-patterned fabric (above left) is not, and there is virtually no difference in the finished chair apart from the legs and the arm supports. The instructions given here are for the simplified version.

Materials and Equipment

¹/₄ in (6mm) hardwood sheet (e.g. jelutong)

³/₃₂ in (2.25mm) hardwood sheet

³/₈ x ¹/₄ in (9 x 6mm) hardwood (e.g. jelutong), for the back legs

Commercially made strip turnings for the front legs

Armrest supports, the top section of two staircase spindles

¹/₁₆ in (1.5mm) thick small piece of hardwood sheet (e.g. jelutong)

Micro wood self-adhesive veneer (see third paragraph, overleaf)

Wood dye

¹/₂ in (12mm) foam

Tacky glue

Fabric as desired

Narrow braid for trimming

For the front legs of the Florentine-patterned chair I used the largest size of commercially made strip-turning available while, for the velvet version, I used turned front legs and arm supports.

Do not use any balsa wood in the construction of this chair: it needs the weight of a heavier wood in the seat, or it will end up top heavy and will overbalance. Balsa is not strong enough for the back either, and the legs would not glue well to it.

The micro wood self-adhesive veneer specified for the edge of the chair seat, is sold in 12 x 14in (30 x 35cm) sheets. I used two shades: two $^1/_{16}$in (1.5mm)

wide strips of light, and one $^1/_{16}$in (1.5mm) wide strip of dark, to contrast. Alternatively, you could use ordinary veneer plus masking tape, veneer tape and contact adhesive, or even a single strip of veneer $^3/_{16}$in (4.5mm) wide.

Construction

1 Prepare the templates 'A' to 'E' below by photocopying them, or tracing them onto thin card, then cut out the shapes.

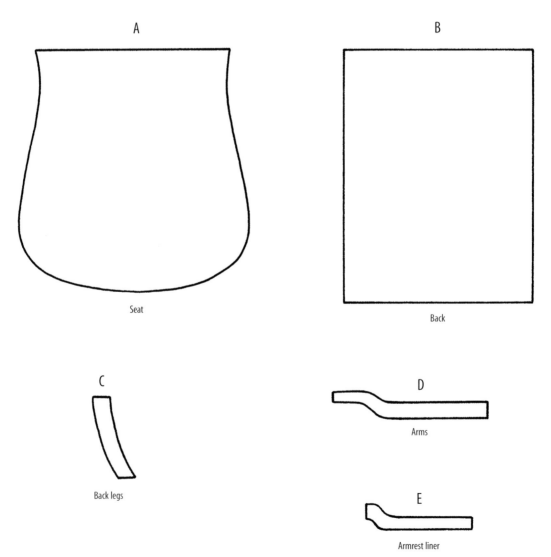

A

Seat

B

Back

C

Back legs

D

Arms

E

Armrest liner

Templates for the wooden framework

126

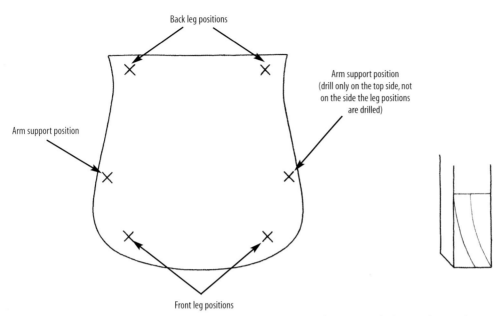

Fig 1 *The positions for the drill holes*

Fig 2 *Draw the leg on the wood using template 'C'*

2 Place seat base template 'A' on ¹/₄in (6mm) hardwood sheet, draw around it, then cut out the shape. Sand the edges smooth and mark in the positions for the drill holes (see Fig 1, above).

3 Drill a hole at each marked position on the underside, and a hole at each arm support position on the upper side (see Fig 1, above).

4 Place the back legs template 'C' on the ³/₈in (9mm) side of the ³/₈ x ¹/₄in (9 x 6mm) hardwood. Cut out the legs, using an electric or hand fretsaw, then use a craft knife and sandpaper to make the legs identical shapes (see Fig 2, above right).

Tip
When cutting veneer, score several shallow cuts against a steel ruler, rather than trying to cut with one stroke. This will give a neater edge and there will be no risk of the knife skidding.

5 Drill the tops of the back legs with a drill bit the same diameter as the cocktail stick dowels. Trim the tapered end from the cocktail stick and discard. Dip the new end into glue and insert into the hole in the top of one leg. Reduce the protruding cocktail stick to ¹/₈in (3mm). Repeat on the second leg. Stain both legs with wood dye and lay aside until needed.

Applying the veneer

6 For the edge of the chair seat, cut two strips of light-coloured veneer and one strip of dark veneer, each no more than ¹/₁₆in (1.5mm) wide. Make sure that the strips are long enough to go around the chair in one piece, to prevent problems in matching up edges, which are nearly always visible. (See 'Tip', left.)

7 If you are using micro wood, it can be cut without preparation, as it has a backing that is peeled off to reveal a sticky adhesive. Peel off the backing from one light strip and stick to the seat around the bottom edge. Stick the dark strip above the light one and the last light strip above that. There will be a ¹/₁₆in (1.5mm) gap at the top, which is correct.

8 If you are using a regular veneer, apply a strip of thin masking tape or paper veneer tape to its surface, then cut through the tape. This will will help you to achieve a smooth-edged cut and hold the veneer together when cutting across the grain.

Spread contact adhesive on the back of the veneer (i.e. not the paper side) and the edge of the chair base. Allow the glue to dry until it is touch dry, about 20 minutes, then attach the veneer as above, paper-side uppermost. With this type of glue you will not be able to move the veneer after attachment, so be careful and precise. Allow an hour or two before removing the paper by dampening and peeling off (in the instance of veneer tape) and leave overnight before using wood stain.

To apply wood stain, put a small amount on a tissue and lightly wipe over the surface.

9 Next, cut the front legs to a length of $^7/_8$in (21mm), then drill and dowel the tops in the same way as the back legs (see step 5, on the previous page). Stain the legs and set aside until needed.

10 Use the arm template 'D' to cut out two arms from $^1/_{16}$in (1.5mm) hardwood, remembering to reverse the template for the second arm. From the same timber, cut four pieces, $^1/_8$in (3mm) wide and the same width as the front of the arm. Glue two blocks, one on top of the other at the front end of each arm. This piece is only to add thickness so that the front of the arm can be rounded to a pleasing shape (see Fig 4, below left).

11 When the glue is dry, sand the front of the arm and the blocks into a nice curved shape (see Fig 4, bottom left).

12 Prepare the arm supports by cutting the top section from two spindles to a length of $^7/_8$in (21mm). Drill and dowel at the bottom (the end that will be in contact with the chair seat), stain, then set aside until needed.

13 Lay the back template on $^3/_{32}$in (2.25mm) hardwood sheet, draw around the shape, then cut out. Sand all the edges smooth. Taper the bottom to a distance of $^1/_4$in (6mm) from the edge (see Fig 5, below right).

Fig 3 Glue the back to the end of the arm

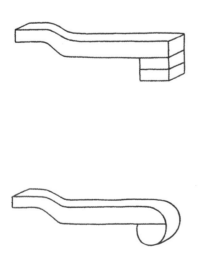

Sand the bottom edge
(shown slightly enlarged for clarity)

Fig 4 Round off carefully with sandpaper

Fig 5 Mark position of taper

14 Glue the back to the rear of the seat base, lining up the bottom edges (see Fig 6, right). Allow to dry completely before proceeding further.

15 Measure $^{7}/_{8}$in (21mm) up the back, from the seat surface. At this point, make a $^{1}/_{16}$in (1.5mm) notch on the back, with the bottom of the notch at the measurement mark (see Fig 6). Repeat on the other side.

16 Glue the arm supports into the holes drilled previously in the seat base. Make sure that they are standing straight, then set aside until the glue is dry.

17 Glue the back of the armrests into the slots cut into the back, then round off the small bit of armrest that is sticking out from the slots at the back (see Fig 7, below). Touch up with wood stain.

18 Very gently ease up the armrest and put a dot of glue on the top of the arm support. Drill through the armrest and into the arm support and insert a dowel. Cut off the excess dowel and sand level with the arm. Touch up with wood stain. This area will not be seen when the upholstery is in position.

19 Glue in the legs and varnish and polish as desired.

Fig 6 Glue the back to the seat

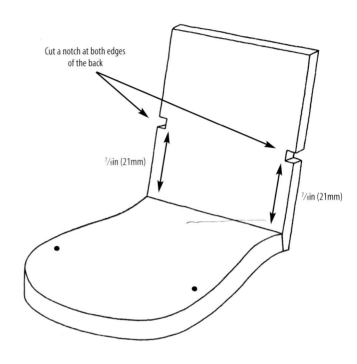

Cut a notch at both edges of the back

$^{7}/_{8}$in (21mm)

$^{7}/_{8}$in (21mm)

Fig 7 Drill and dowel through the top of the armrest and into the arm support

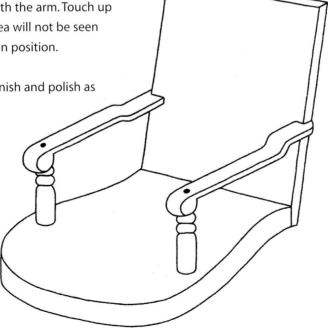

The completed framework

Upholstery

Fig 8 *Trim the liner to the exact size as the inside back, then cut a piece of sponge the same size as the liner*

Use the back and seat templates 'A' and 'B', used for the construction of the chair as upholstery liners. In addition, photocopy or trace the back template 'B' again to use as an outer-back upholstery liner.

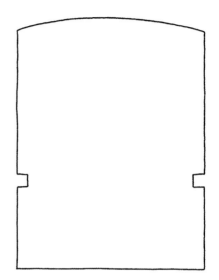

1 Try-fit the inner back liner against the inside back of the chair. Trim to fit exactly.

2 Cut a piece of foam using the inner-back liner as a template (see Fig 8, on right).

3 Cut a piece of fabric 1in (24mm) larger on all sides than the liner (see Fig 9, below).

4 Turn up the bottom edge of the fabric and glue to the back of the liner. Cut the fold at each bottom corner (Fig 9).

Fig 9 *Turn up the bottom edge of the fabric and glue to the bottom of the card, then snip the folds*

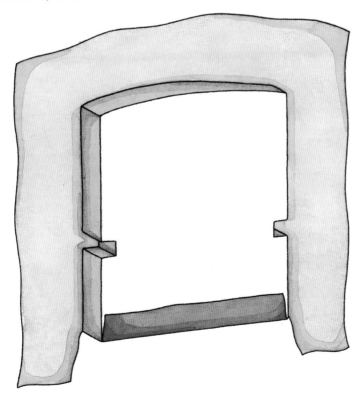

5 Glue the back of the liner to the inner back of the chair. Very carefully snip into the fabric at the armrest positions (see Fig 10, right).

6 At each side, take the fabric from below the snip under the armrest, and glue it to the back of the chair. Repeat with the fabric above the armrest. Spread glue on the fabric at the top edge and begin folding it to the back, easing the fabric around the curves by pinching it into small triangles. Cut these off when the glue is dry, to minimize the thickness, but do not pull the fabric too tight, or it will end up uneven (see Fig 11, below left).

7 Cut the small overhang at each bottom side edge to an angle, turn the raw edge under a small amount, then glue the overhang to the side of the chair.

8 Try-fit the seat-base liner around the arm supports and trim to fit, as necessary.

9 Cut a piece of foam using the seat liner as a template. Glue the liner to the foam.

Fig 10 Glue the card to the back of the chair. Snip into the fabric at the armrest positions

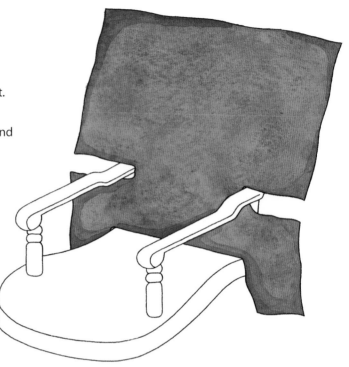

Fig 11 Bring the excess fabric round to the back of the chair, then glue it in position

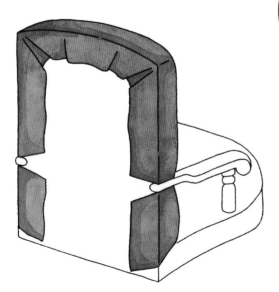

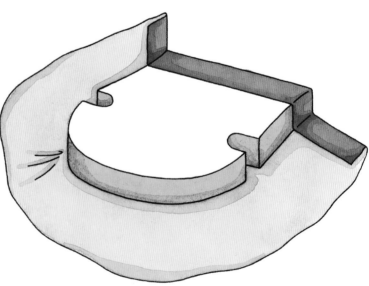

Fig 12 Fold in the corners

10 Cut a piece of fabric 1in (24mm) larger all around than the foam/liner (see Fig 12, facing page).

11 At the back bottom edge turn under the fabric and glue to the reverse of the card. Where the fold at each side was created, fold in each side, then fold over the top of the fabric to neaten each corner (see Fig 13, on right). Glue or sew to secure.

12 Glue the seat base in position. Cut the fabric at the arm supports to divide.

13 Above the veneer, where you left a narrow strip of bare wood (see step 7 of 'Applying the veneer', page127), run a line of glue from the back to the arm support. Then, using the flat, blunt tool, position the fabric over the line of glue, pushing it into the glue line and creasing the fabric above the veneer. Fold back the fabric, then wipe off any glue that has oozed out onto the veneer (see Fig 14, below).

14 Do the same around the front edge easing in any fullness of fabric at the curves as you go.

Fig 14 Glue the fabric to the wood above the veneer

Fig 13 Gluing fabric to the card at the back bottom edge

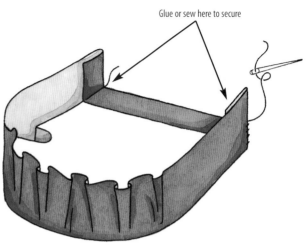

Glue or sew here to secure

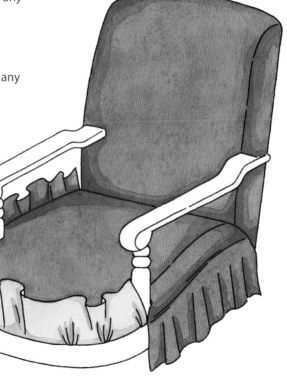

Fold back the fabric and clean any glue off the veneer

Fig 15 *Trim the excess fabric around the top of the veneer*

Fig 16 *Covering the armrests*

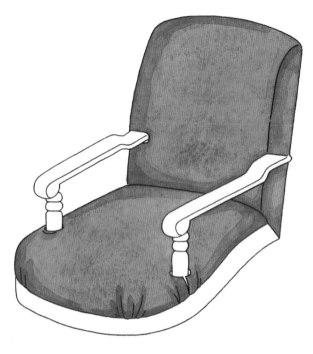

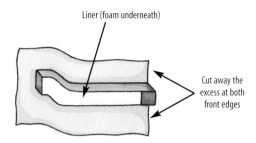

Liner (foam underneath)

Cut away the excess at both front edges

Fig 17

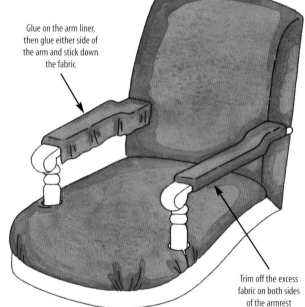

Glue on the arm liner, then glue either side of the arm and stick down the fabric

Trim off the excess fabric on both sides of the armrest

15 When the glue is dry, take a sharp craft knife and trim off the excess fabric at the crease above the veneer (see Fig 15, above).

16 Cut a piece of ¼in (6mm) foam the same size as the armrest liners, making sure that you have a left and a right arm liner/foam. Glue the foam to the liners.

17 Cut a piece of fabric ¼in (6mm) larger all around than the liners (Fig 16, top right). Fold under the fabric at the fronts of the liners and glue to the back of the card liner.

18 Glue the liner to the top of the armrests, making sure it covers the dowel positions. Run a line of glue along each side edge of the armrest and fold down the fabric over it. When the glue is dry, trim the excess fabric level with the bottom edge of the armrests.

Fig 18 *Glue the card liner to the reverse of the fabric, then fold over the excess to the back of the card*

19 Trim the back liner to fit just inside the back shape. Cover with fabric and turn under the excess to the reverse of the card (see Fig 18, bottom right, facing page). Remove the folds created at the bottom corners when doing this.

20 Glue the covered liner to the back of the chair, rubbing the edges with your flat tool to neaten. Fold under and glue the excess under the chair (see Fig 19, right).

21 To finish, trim the chair with narrow braid, around the seat above the veneer and around the arm edges.

Fig 19 *Glue the covered liner to the back of the chair, folding the excess under the bottom of the seat*

Wing Chair

This chair is difficult to date. Many versions of the wing chair exist, dating back to the time of Thomas Chippendale in the eighteenth century. The version shown here is a bit of a mixture of styles, but it has recognizable features that give a reassuring feeling of familiarity.

Materials and Equipment

Card for templates

$^{1}/_{4}$ in (6mm) jelutong or balsa sheet

$^{3}/_{8}$ in (9mm) balsa dowel

$^{1}/_{16}$ in (1.5mm) plywood light or heavy mount board

$^{3}/_{8}$ x $^{1}/_{4}$ in (9 x 6mm) pine strip or hardwood

$^{3}/_{8}$ in (9mm) square hardwood (jelutong, mahogany or walnut)

10 x 2mm pine strip (only sold in metric) or other hardwood (not balsa)

2 cabriole legs as template, or 2 ready-made miniature legs

PVA wood glue

Stiff fabric for the seat well (see page 7)

Dried silver sand (see page 4)

Wood stain and varnish

$^{1}/_{4}$ in (6mm) and $^{1}/_{2}$ in (12mm) foam

2 sq. ft (60 sq. cm) gloving leather

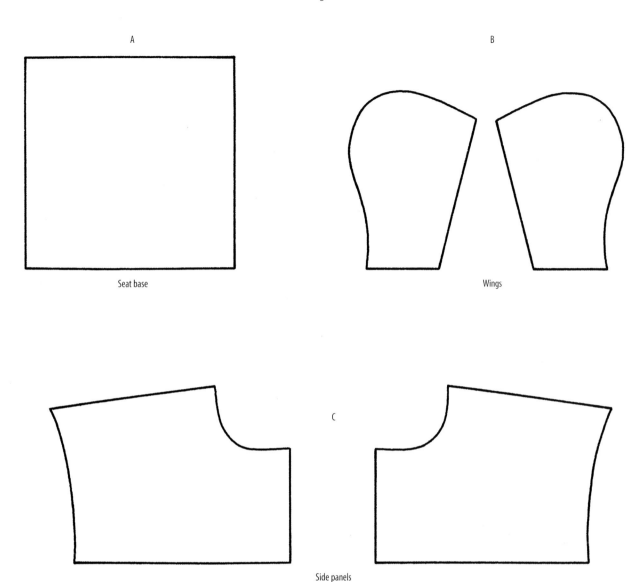

A

Seat base

B

Wings

C

Side panels

Templates for the wooden framework

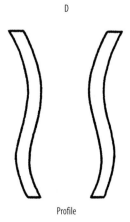

D

Profile

Prepare templates 'A' to 'G' as accurately as possible, by tracing or photocopying them onto card. Accuracy at this stage will make the final fitting together easier, and the templates can be re-used to make more chairs exactly the same size as the original.

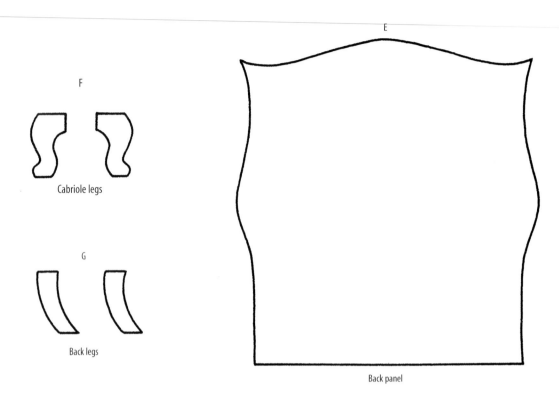

F

Cabriole legs

G

Back legs

E

Back panel

Templates for the wooden framework

Construction

Preparing the wing shapes

1 Lay template 'B' (wings) on ¼in (6mm) jelutong or balsa sheet, with the direction of the wood grain as shown in Fig 1, right. Draw around each one.

2 Place templates 'D' (profile) on the back end grain (i.e. the flat surface at the back) of the cut out wing shapes 'B', making sure that they are mirror images, as indicated in Fig 2 (top diagram, facing page). Draw around both as accurately as possible then, using a hand or electric fretsaw, cut along each drawn line, keeping the fretsaw as level as possible.

Note

The direction of the wood grain is indicated by arrows on the diagrams

Direction of wood grain

B

B

wood

***Fig 1** Cut out, using a hand or electric fretsaw*

Fig 2 *Cut along the dotted lines of profile 'D'*

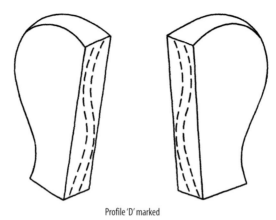

Profile 'D' marked

3 Fig 3 (right) shows the shape you will end up with, each one a mirror image of the other. Round off the edges with sandpaper to make the inside face gently curved. Do not round off the back flat edges. Flatten the flared-out bottom edge on both sides. Set aside until needed.

Preparation of the sides

1 Draw around both parts 'C' (side panels), onto ¹⁄₄in (6mm) jelutong or balsa sheet, following the layout shown in Fig 4, below. Cut out the shapes.

Fig 3

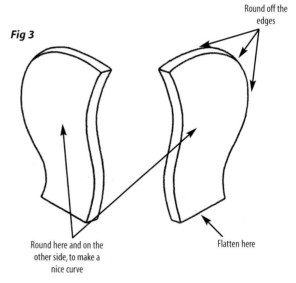

Round off the edges

Round here and on the other side, to make a nice curve

Flatten here

Fig 4 *Draw around template 'C' and cut out*

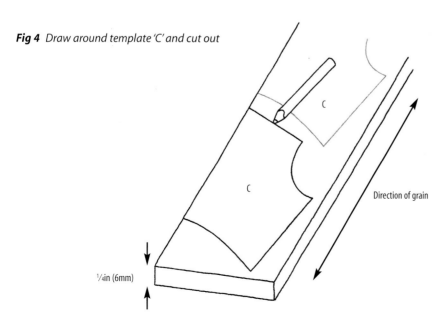

C

C

Direction of grain

¹⁄₄in (6mm)

Fig 5 *Mark both on one side (mirror image)*

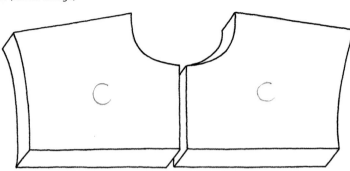

2 Mark both parts 'C' on the outer face so that when the arm roll is attached there is no risk of ending up with two right or two left sides (Fig 5, above).

3 Cut two lengths of balsa dowel 1⁵/₈in (41mm). Flatten one side of each piece of dowel equally (see Fig 6, below).

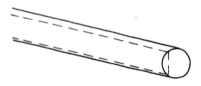

Fig 6 *Flatten one side*

4 Glue the dowel to the outside face of both side parts 'C', ensuring that you have a right and a left piece before the glue dries (see Fig 7, below left). Wipe of any excess glue that comes out from under the arm roll. Set aside to dry completely.

5 Using a craft knife, shave away the top flat edge of the side shape, so that it curves gently towards the arm roll (see Fig 8, below). Finish off with sandpaper.

6 Using a craft knife, shave away the back of the arm roll until it also curves gently. Round off with sandpaper (see Fig 9, below right).

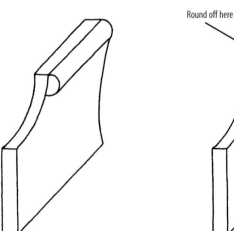

Round off here

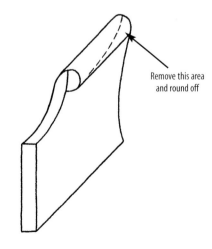

Remove this area and round off

Fig 7 *Glue the dowel to the outer face*   **Fig 8** *Shave the top flat edge*   **Fig 9** *Curve the back of the arm roll*

Fig 10 *Cutting a slot in the side assembly*

Fig 11 *Gluing the wing into the slot*

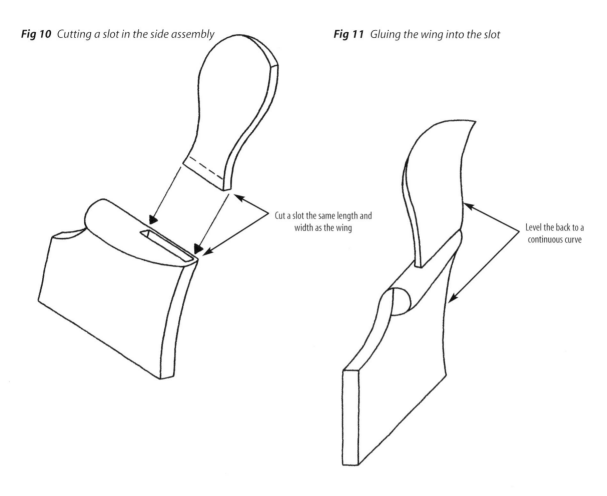

Cut a slot the same length and width as the wing

Level the back to a continuous curve

Putting the side parts together

1 Cut a slot in the side assembly the length of the base of the wing and ¹⁄₈in (3mm) wide and ¹⁄₈in (3mm) deep (see Fig 10, above).

2 Glue the wing shape into the slot. Make sure, before the glue dries, that the back of the wing and the side assembly line up exactly (see Fig 11, above right). Set aside to dry completely, preferably overnight.

Tip

When constructing the seat base, tape together two strips of wood of the same size and cut as one. This will ensure that each pair of sides is precisely the same length. But note that the parts from the long sides, both upper and lower set, are the same length, while the side parts are not.

Seat construction

It is important to lay out the seat base parts on top of template 'A' (page 137) to check the sizes, particularly of the short side parts. If you have used a different size of wood to that specified, these side parts will be too short. To rectify this, lay the front and back long strips in position on the seat base template 'A', then measure between them accurately. This will give you the size to cut the short side parts.

1 From 10 x 2mm pine strip, cut two pieces 2³⁄₁₆in (56mm) and two pieces 1³⁄₈in (35mm) long, for the lower base.

2 From ³⁄₈ x ¹⁄₄in (9 x 6mm) pine strip, cut two pieces 2³⁄₁₆in (56mm) and two pieces 1³⁄₄in (44mm) long, for the upper seat base.

Fig 12 *Arrange the pieces for the seat base as shown*

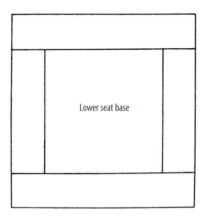

Lower seat base

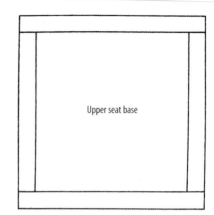

Upper seat base

3 Lay out the cut pieces for the lower and upper seat bases on a sheet of waxed paper, as shown above. Glue, then allow to dry thoroughly before handling.

4 Glue the upper seat base on top of the lower seat base, squaring up the edges so that they line up exactly (see Fig 13, right). Cover with waxed paper, then place a heavy object, such as a book, on top of the paper. Make sure that the parts do not slip apart while you are doing this. Set aside to dry.

Fig 13 *Glue in this manner*

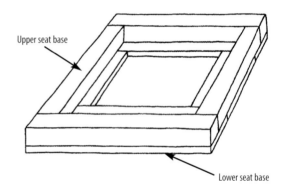

Upper seat base

Lower seat base

Assembling the seat and sides

1 Glue both side assemblies onto the seat base, making sure that the back of the side assembly is level with the back of the seat base.

2 Put two large pins into each side to hold them in position while they dry (see Fig 14, right). Alternatively tape or clamp in position. It is essential to allow the glue to dry properly on these parts, otherwise they will move when the back is added.

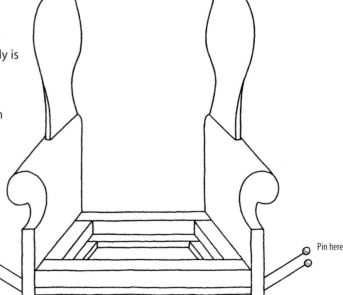

Pin here

Pin here

Fig 14 *Pin, tape or clamp sides in position, until the glue is dry*

Adding the back

1 Draw around back shape 'E' onto ¹⁄₁₆in (1.5mm) plywood, with the grain of the wood running in the direction shown in Fig 15, right. The grain direction is important, otherwise the wood will not flex correctly to fit the curvature of the back of the chair. Cut out the back shape.

2 Glue the back in position, lining up the bottom edges and overlapping the sides. Hold in position with masking tape around the back curve of the side assemblies (see Fig 16, below right). Do not remove the tape until the glue is thoroughly dried or the back and the chair will spring apart.

3 When the glue is properly dried, trim the excess back panel at each side with a sharp knife.

N.B. The back template is made larger purposely, to take into account variations in curvature when finishing the wing shapes.

Attaching the legs

1 See instructions for cutting the cabriole legs on page 10. After cutting out, sand away the corners on the legs and feet, both back and front, so that the legs are nicely rounded along their length and around the feet. Do not sand the flat surfaces, as these are needed to attach the legs to the seat base

2 Take a drill bit the same thickness as the cocktail sticks (measure this with the blunt end of the drill, as this is the size of hole the drill bit will cut), and set the bit into a pin vice or electric drill. Drill a ¹⁄₈in (3mm) deep hole in the top of the cabriole leg.

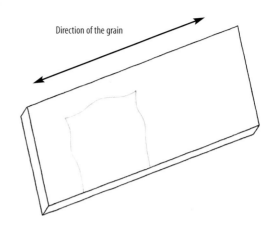
Direction of the grain

Fig 15 *Place the template in the direction of the grain, then cut out*

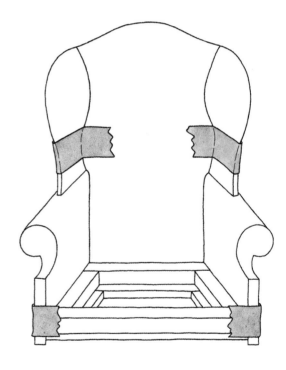

Fig 16 *Tapes holding the back in position while the glue dries*

Tip

To prevent drilling straight through your precious leg and ruining it, wrap a piece of masking tape around the drill bit to mark the depth you want the drill to go, and don't push the drill bit into the wood past your tape marker.

Fig 17 *Dowelling the front, cabriole, legs*   **Fig 18** *Cutting the back legs*

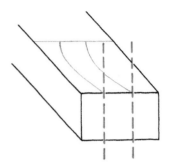

3 Put a dot of wood glue into the hole just drilled, cut off the tapered end of the cocktail stick and discard. Place the cut end into the drilled hole and cut off the excess stick, leaving $1/8$ in (3mm) (see Fig 17, above).

The back legs

1 Take some $3/8$ x $1/4$ in (9 x 6mm) hardwood and measure $3/8$ in (9mm) along one side. Place the back leg template 'G' (see page 138) on this and draw around on one side only.

2 Cut along each of the drawn lines (see Fig 18, above).

3 Sand the leg smooth.

4 Drill and dowel the tops as with the cabriole legs.

5 Finish both sets of legs with wood stain. Do not varnish the legs until they are applied to the chair, as the varnish would inhibit the join between leg and chair.

The completed framework

Attaching the legs to the chair

1 At each corner drill a hole on the base of the seat $\frac{1}{4}$in (6mm) from the front and the same distance from the side; the hole should be the same size as the hole drilled for the dowels in the top of the legs.

2 Put a small dot of glue inside the drill holes and spread a little on the top of the legs.

3 Fix the legs in position, making sure that the rounded part of the leg faces the outer corners of the chair.

4 Finish the legs with varnish or French polish, and the chair is then ready for upholstery.

Additional templates

H

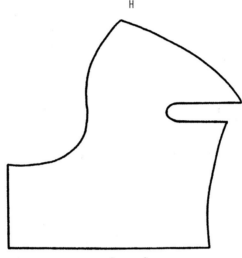

Arm cover liner

I

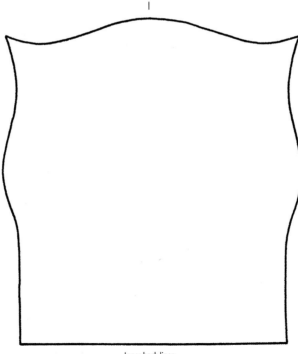

Inner back liner

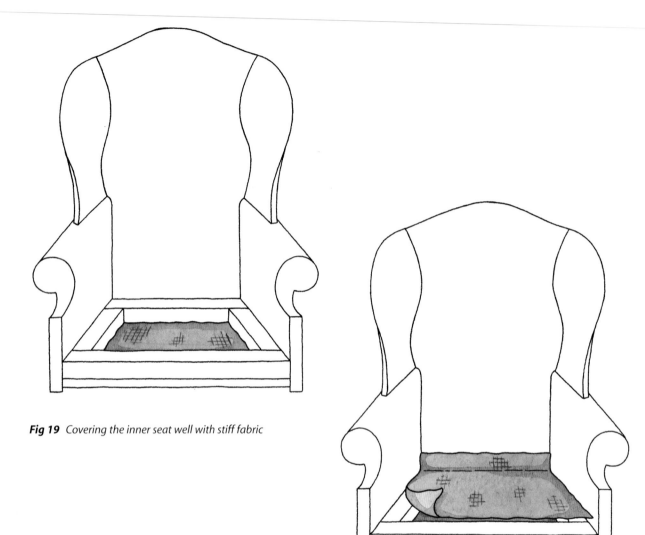

Fig 19 *Covering the inner seat well with stiff fabric*

Fig 20 *Covering the seat surface with stiff fabric. Do not glue down at the sides and front*

Upholstery

Cut out a second set of templates from thin card. Make two of the back panel 'E', two of the wing shapes 'B', two of the sides 'C' and two templates 'H' and 'I' on the previous page. These shapes will act as the linings for the upholstery. I have purposely not drawn them exact size because of variations between my knife and sandpaper shaping and yours. Therefore all the shapes will need to be trimmed to size. Leave this trimming until you need to use them, or the added bulk of the upholstery will make them very inaccurate.

Before starting to upholster, cut a piece of the stiff fabric (not leather) to fit the inside recess of the chair seat and glue it into position (see Fig 19, above). When the glue is dry, coat the fabric with neat PVA, to make it impervious to the sand.

Cut a second piece of stiff fabric to fit the whole surface of the seat, but trim 1/8 in (3mm) of fabric from the front edge. Glue only along the back edge at this stage, and fix in place (see Fig 20, above right).

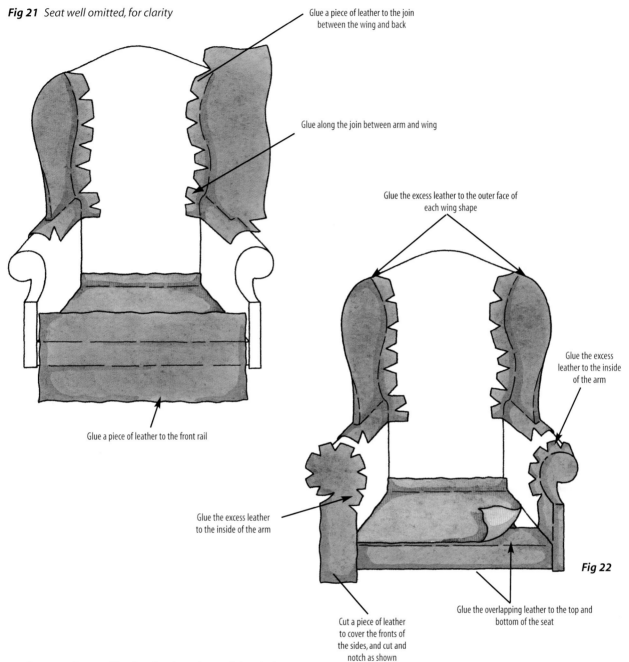

Fig 21 *Seat well omitted, for clarity*

Glue a piece of leather to the join between the wing and back

Glue along the join between arm and wing

Glue the excess leather to the outer face of each wing shape

Glue the excess leather to the inside of the arm

Glue a piece of leather to the front rail

Glue the excess leather to the inside of the arm

Fig 22

Cut a piece of leather to cover the fronts of the sides, and cut and notch as shown

Glue the overlapping leather to the top and bottom of the seat

1 Cut two pieces of leather for the wings of the chair, at least 1in (25mm) larger all around than the wing itself; notch along one side. Glue to the back, as close to the wing joint as you can get (Fig 21, above). Do not get any glue on the wing, or the leather will not stretch.

2 Cut a third piece of leather to fit the front of the seat edge, allowing ½in (12mm) overhang at the top and bottom. Glue down the top overhang of leather to the top surface of the seat. Fill the cavity with dry

sand and glue down the fabric at the sides and front. Cut two more pieces of fabric, long enough to cover the front of the arms. Notch as shown in the Fig 22, above. Glue in position, trimming off any excess as you go. Apply glue to the leather to cover the wings, not the wing itself; stretch the leather over the wings and fix to the outer sides. Pinch the leather and trim off the excess as you go.

Fig 23 *Covering the inside back*

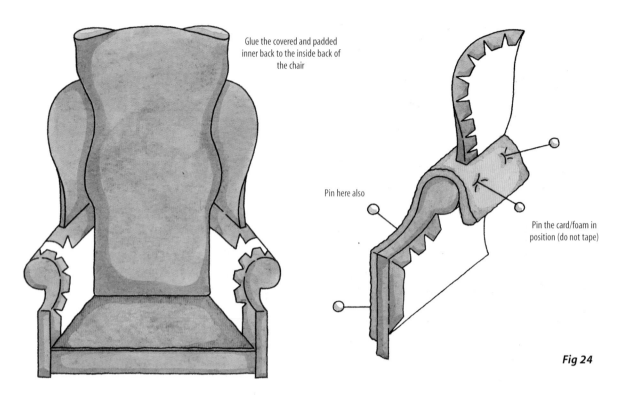

Glue the covered and padded
inner back to the inside back of
the chair

Pin here also

Pin the card/foam in
position (do not tape)

Fig 24

3 Trim the lining back shape to fit the inside back exactly, then cut a piece of ½in (12mm) foam to the same size. Cut a piece of leather large enough to overlap both the card and foam all around. Lay the leather right side down on a flat surface, centralize the foam piece on top and, on top of that, the card liner. Spread glue along the bottom edge of the card, fold up the leather, and glue down. Repeat on both side edges, stretching the leather as you go, but not too tightly. Tidy up any excess on the back, then glue the shape to the inside back of the chair, taking care not to get any glue on the leather surface (see Fig 23, above left).

4 Trim the inner arm template 'H' to fit the inside of the arm assembly. The cut-out 'U' shape fits around the base of the wing where it is joined to the arm. Curve the card over the arm roll, but do

not flatten out the curve. Cut a piece of ¼in (6mm) foam to fit the card shape, allowing a little extra on the arm roll. Do not stretch the foam, or it will flatten (see Fig 24, above right).

5 Cut two pieces of leather large enough to overlap the card/foam by ¼in (6mm) all around, except on the arm-roll edge, where it must overlap by ½in (12mm). Remember to reverse the process on the second piece of leather, so that you have a left and right (mirror image). Lay the leather pieces face down, then place the foam on top and the card on top of the foam. Cut triangular notches around the front curve and around the 'U' shape. Fold up the notched edges and glue to the card (see Fig 25, top left, on the facing page). Take special care to keep the leather smooth around the 'U' shape. Lay aside until needed.

Fig 25 *Notch the leather, taking care to keep it smooth*

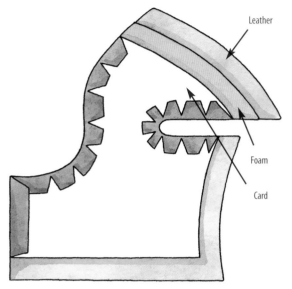

Leather

Foam

Card

Fig 26 *Attaching the outer wing covers*

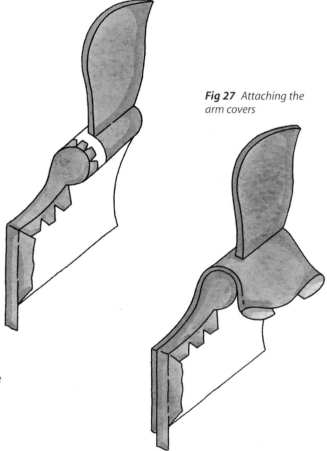

Fig 27 *Attaching the arm covers*

The outer wings

1 Trim the wing-shape templates 'B' to fit the outside wing. Trim a further $^1/_8$in (3mm) from the curved edge. Ensure that you have a right and left (mirror image) before continuing, then cut two pieces of leather $^1/_4$in (6mm) larger all around than your card shapes. Centre the card shape on the back of the leather and glue in position.

2 Cut triangular notches along the curved edge only, then fold over the notched edge and glue down. Spread glue over the back of the finished shape, making sure that the glue goes right up to the curved edge. Glue in position $^1/_8$in (3mm) from the curved edge of the wing. Glue the excess at the bottom edge over the arm roll, and the excess at the back around to the back of the chair. Using the flat-edged tool, rub over the curved edge of the wing to flatten and tidy up the join; this forces the two leather surfaces together and nobody will be able to tell that the seam isn't sewn (see Fig 26, above).

Applying the arm covering

1 Take the arm-roll shapes prepared in steps 4 and 5 on the facing page, spread glue over the back and position them inside the side assembly and around the base of the wing. Take care not to get any glue on the leather surface (see Fig 25, above).

2 Fold back the leather over the arm and trim any excess foam and card protruding past the arm roll, but do not cut the leather back yet. Smooth the leather over the arm roll and hold it in position, now trim the leather until there is a $^1/_4$in (6mm) overhang past the arm roll (see Fig 27, above right).

Fig 28 Attaching the outer side cover

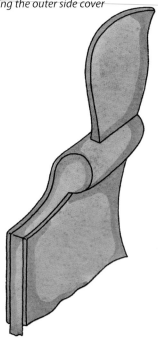

6 Notch around the curved edge. Fold over and glue down on the front, top and curved edges only.

7 Glue the covered shapes in position on the outside of the chair sides. Use your flat-bladed tool to rub the front edge, curving it as before, and to push the top curved edge under the arm roll.

8 Glue the excess leather at the back, apart from the bottom, to the back of the chair. Do not glue down the excess at the bottom at this stage (Fig 28, left).

Fitting the back

1 Trim the back card lining 'E' to fit the back of the chair, less ¹⁄₈in (3mm) on the sides and top edges.

2 Cut a piece of leather larger than the card by ¹⁄₄in (6mm) on all sides.

3 Glue the card shape to the leather.

4 Spread glue on the leather overhang on the top and sides fold over the sides and the top, pinching at the top corners to mitre them to get a flat finish (see Fig 29, below). Set aside.

Fig 29 Glue the card to the reverse of the leather

3 Run a line of glue under the arm where it joins the chair side, then force the excess leather into the join with the flat-bladed tool. Be careful here: if you use too much pressure, you may break the arm roll; far better to start off a little gently than have to repair the arm. Don't try to push too much leather into the join – if you have difficulty fitting it in, trim a little more off the edge.

4 Trim the outer-side card shape 'C' to fit closely under the arm roll and ¹⁄₈in (3mm) less than the front curve and the front edge. To do this line up the card shape with the bottom edge of the chair side and the front straight edge, then hold in position while you pencil in the front curve. Cut around the front curve, inside your pencil line. Reposition the card shape, lining up the bottom edges and the front curve, and hold in position, using your flat-bladed tool to crease the card to the curvature of the arm roll. Trim to the creased line. Repeat on the second side.

5 Cut a piece of leather ¹⁄₄in (6mm) larger all around than the card liner. Centre the card on the back of the leather and glue down.

Finishing the back

Fig 30 *Tidy up the top edge*

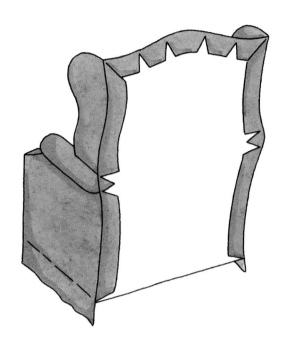

1 On the top unfinished edge of the chair, trim off any excess foam, leaving it sticking up slightly.

2 Snip off the fold of leather that was created when the inside back was covered.

3 Fold over the excess leather, pulling slightly, to create a nice smooth shape on the top edge.

4 Glue down the excess leather pinching up triangles of leather as you go to take up the excess.

5 Cut off the triangles and tidy up any other bulky areas (see Fig 30, top right).

6 Glue on the back liner (see Fig 31, below). Tidy up by rubbing with your flat-bladed tool to flatten the joins. When the glue is dry cut off the little folds on the bottom edge of the chair that were created when the card liners were covered. Fold under the excess leather and fit around the legs. Finally, cut a piece of fabric to fit the underneath of the chair; this must fit around the inside of the legs so that there are no edges of leather visible.

Fig 31 *Glue on the back liner*

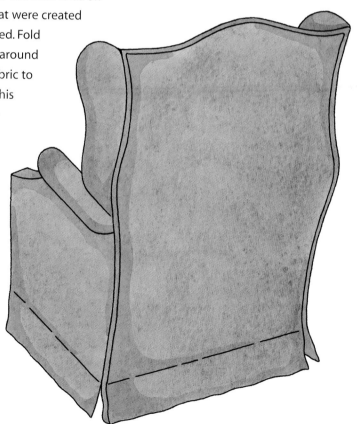

Make the cushion following the directions given on page
9 and using seat template 'A', on page 137, trimmed to fit.
Place the cushion on the chair with the seam at the back.

Give the entire chair surface a light buffing with
a soft clean cloth, but do not use leather dressing,
as that would make the leather dark and patchy.
If necessary use a little bit of neutral shoe cream.

Your chair is now complete.

'Gothic' Chair

This variation on the wing chair project in the previous chapter may also feel familiar, although I don't think I have ever seen it in a book on antique furniture. I have, however, spotted it in several of the Hammer movies of the late 1960s and 70s, so Dracula rides again, because I've pinched his chair! It could be the result of someone's idea of a chair from the Victorian Gothic period and pure invention for the movie set but, whatever it is, it is easily adapted from the wing chair design.

Materials and Equipment	
Card for templates	PVA wood glue
¹/₄ in (6mm) jelutong or balsa sheet	Stiff fabric for the seat well (see page 7)
³/₈ in (9mm) balsa dowel	Dried silver sand (see page 4)
¹/₁₆ in (1.5mm) plywood light or heavy mount-board	Wood stain and varnish
³/₈ x ¹/₄ in (10 x 6mm) pine strip or hardwood	Sandpaper
³/₈ in (9mm) square jelutong or other hardwood, e.g. mahogany or walnut	¹/₄ in (6mm) and ¹/₂ in (12mm) foam
2 x 10mm pine strip or other hardwood (not balsa)	³/₁₆ in (4.5mm) balsa or jelutong
Two cabriole legs as template, or two ready-made miniature legs	2 extra short lengths of balsa dowel
	Devoré silk velvet

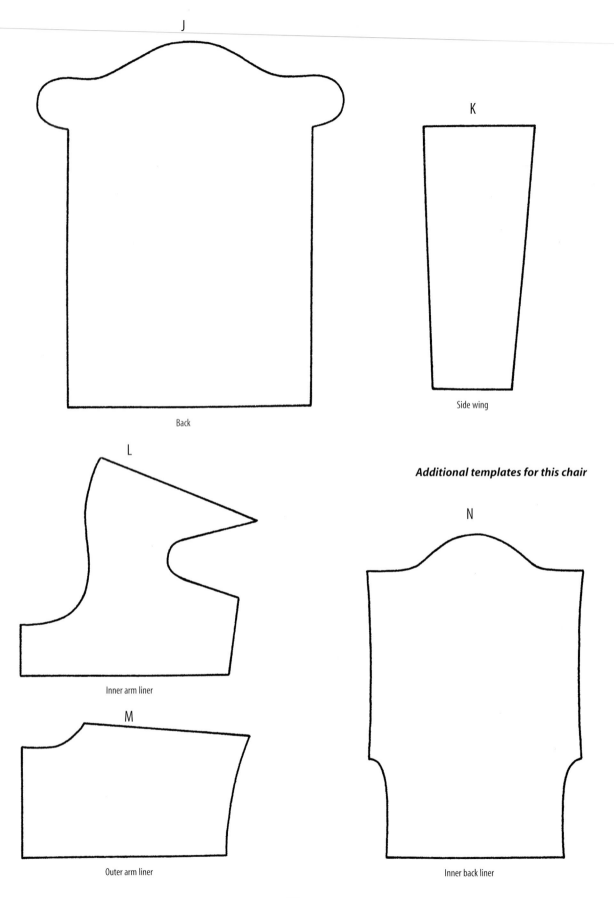

J

K

Side wing

Back

L

Inner arm liner

Additional templates for this chair

N

M

Outer arm liner

Inner back liner

Fig 1 The cut out wing shapes

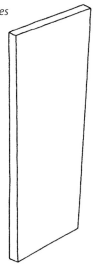

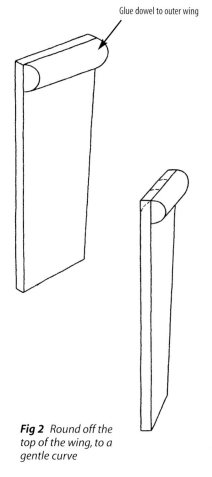

Glue dowel to outer wing

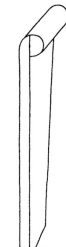

Construction

Use the wing chair templates on pages 137–8 for constructing the seat base, sides and legs. Only the back and wings are different for this project and there are additional templates for these on the facing page.

1 Make up the seat and sides using the instructions given for the wing chair on pages 139–42.

2 Photocopy or trace the templates on the facing page onto thin card. Make two copies of the back, four copies of the side wings, two inner arm liners, two outer arm liners and one inner back liner.

3 Take one of the side-wing templates 'K' and draw around it twice onto $^3/_{16}$in (4.5mm) balsa or jelutong sheet. Cut out the shape, then set aside the template for use later with the back, inner arm and outer arm upholstery liners made in step 2.

4 Cut two pieces of $^3/_8$in (9mm) balsa dowel $1^1/_8$in (27mm) long. Flatten one side and glue to the top outer edge of the wing sides, ensuring that you have a right and a left side (see Fig 1, above).

Fig 2 Round off the top of the wing, to a gentle curve

5 Using a craft knife and sandpaper, round off the top inner edge of the wing side so that it curves into the dowel (see Fig 2, above).

6 Cut a rebate using a craft knife $^1/_{16}$in (1.5mm) deep and $^1/_{16}$in (1.5mm) high on the bottom edge of both sides of each wing shape (see Fig 3, overleaf).

7 At the top back edge of the chair arms, cut a slot $^1/_{16}$in (1.5mm) wide, $^1/_{16}$in (1.5mm) deep and $^7/_8$in (21mm) long (see Fig 4, below left).

8 Run wood glue into the slot and insert the rebated end of the wing (see Fig 5, below right). Repeat on the second side. Make sure that the roll top faces outwards on each side arm. Set aside to allow the glue to dry completely.

9 When the glue is dry, glue one side-assembly to each side of the seat lining up the back and bottom edges. Clamp or tape in position. Set aside until the glue is dry.

10 Level off the back edge of each side with sandpaper, so that there is a continuous flat surface from the top roll to the seat base.

11 Draw around the back template onto heavy mount board or $^1/_{16}$in (1.5mm) plywood light. Cut out.

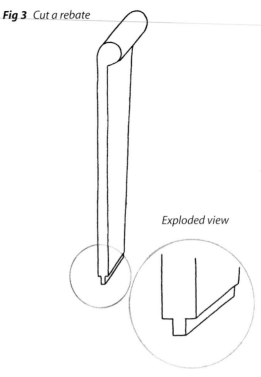

Fig 3 *Cut a rebate*

Exploded view

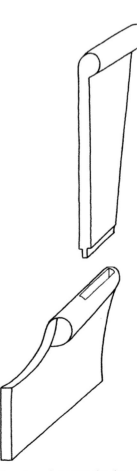

Fig 4 *Cut a slot in the top of the arm*

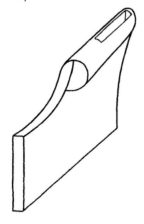

Fig 5 *Glue the wing rebate into the slot cut in the top of the arm*

156

12 Glue the back in position, lining up the bottom edge and top wing rolls, then tape or clamp in position. If the back needs some trimming, this is best done after it is in position and the glue is dry. Sand the top edge of the back and the side edges, then give the rest of the surfaces a light sanding.

13 Prepare and attach the legs using the instructions given for the Wing Chair (see page 143–5).

The completed framework

Upholstery

I used a ¼ in (6mm) foam to upholster the inner sides and inner wings of this example, because I like the softness. The inner area of the chair would look larger if a thinner foam or a fine cotton batting (primarily used for quilting) were used, and this would be helpful if you intend to sit a doll in the chair.

Because I love rich textiles, the fabric I used is a hand-dyed, devoré silk velvet. To achieve the light and dark shadowing shown on my example, simply vary the direction of the velvet pile. Alternatively, a printed or plain velvet would look just as good, or even a 'tapestry' type fabric.

This chair took one A4 piece of patterned fabric and the same quantity of plain. The method for the upholstery is exactly the same as that for the wing chair, except for the covering on the wings (see pages 147–51).

Covering the wings

The wings are covered before the inner side arms.

1 Cut a piece of fabric to cover the front flat edges of the wings and clip into the corner beneath the rolls.

2 Spread glue on the inner and outer faces of the wood and fold back the fabric onto the glue, easing in the fullness over the curve by pinching it into triangles. Allow the glue to dry before snipping off the triangles (see Fig 6, top right).

3 Cut a piece of foam 1in (24mm) longer than the inner wing liners, then cut a piece of fabric 1in (24mm) larger all around than the foam.

4 Pin the bottom of the liner to the bottom of the wing, and taking the card over the top roll, pin to the underside. Glue the foam to the card, removing and replacing the pins as you go. Do not stretch the foam over the roll, just allow it to curve gently. Leave alone until the glue is dry.

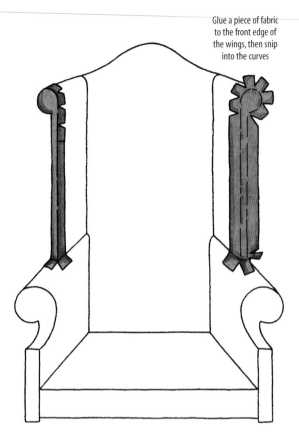

Glue a piece of fabric to the front edge of the wings, then snip into the curves

Fig 6 *Glue the excess fabric onto the inner and outer face of the wing*

5 When the glue is dry remove the liner from the chair, and you should find that it retains the shape of the curve (Fig 7, facing page). Centralize the foam over the reverse of the fabric, turn over the excess at each long edge, and glue to the reverse of the card liner.

6 Trim the excess fabric away from each corner, where the fabric was folded over the card (Fig 8, facing page).

7 Spread glue over the back of the wing upholstery and position on the inside wing. Pin in place until the glue is dry.

8 Glue the excess fabric at the base of the wing to the inside of the arm assembly (see Fig 9, facing page).

Fig 7 *When the glue is dry, the liner retains its shape*

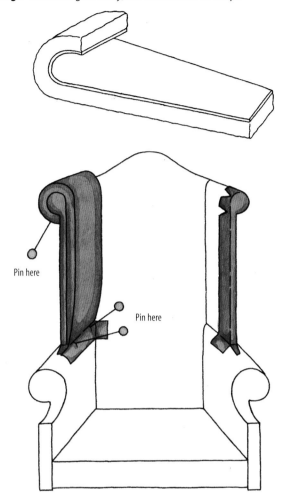

Pin here

Pin here

Fig 9 *Adding the inner upholstery to the wing*

Fig 8 *Cut the fabric at each corner as in step 1, facing page*

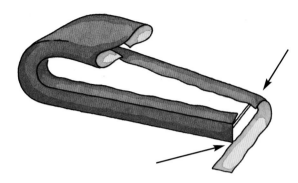

9 Trim off any excess liner, foam and fabric until the liner and foam just fit under the top roll but the fabric remains a little longer, to allow it to be pushed into the join between the roll and wing on its own.

10 Cut two card wing shapes 'K' to fit between the top of the arm roll and the underside of the wing top roll.

11 Cut a piece of fabric ¼ in (6mm) larger all around than the card liner trimmed in the step above. Centre and glue the liner to the reverse of the fabric. On the front and top edge only, fold over and glue the excess fabric to the reverse of the card liner mitring the front corner. Trim away the folded fabric formed at the top and bottom corners (see Figs 10 and 11, below).

Fig 10 *Centre the card liner on the reverse of the fabric*

Fig 11 *Fold over the excess fabric and glue down*

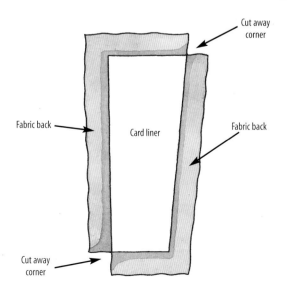

Cut away corner

Fabric back

Card liner

Fabric back

Cut away corner

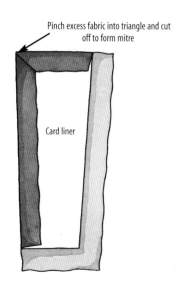

Pinch excess fabric into triangle and cut off to form mitre

Card liner

12 Glue the covered liner under the top roll, so that the fabric-covered edge is at the front. Glue the excess at the bottom over the arm roll, and the excess at the back around to the back of the chair (see Fig 12, right).

13 To complete the chair, follow the upholstery for the wing chair project from step 2 (page 147), omitting the instructions for covering the wings.

Fig 12 *Covering the wings*

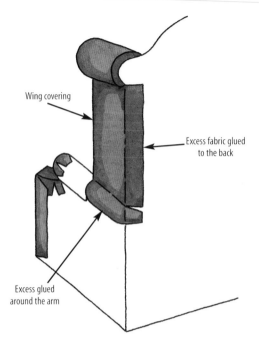

Wing covering

Excess fabric glued to the back

Excess glued around the arm

Suppliers

UNITED KINGDOM

Leather and foam sheeting

SM Upholstery Ltd
212 Whitchurch Road
Cardiff
CF14 3NB

Tel: 02920 619813

Fabrics

Hilary Williams
The Silk Route
Cross Cottage
Cross Lane
Frimley Green
Surrey
GU16 6LN

Tel: 01252 835781

Cabriole and turned legs

McQueenie Miniatures
15 Wensum Way
Belton
Norfolk
NR31 9NY

e-mail: B.Mc@btinternet.com

Tools

Squires Model and Craft Tools
100 London Road
Bognor Regis
West Sussex
PO21 1DD

Tel: 01243 842424

Wood supplies

Any model-making supply store (see Yellow Pages)

USA

Tools

The General Store
N1246 Thrush Drive
Greenville
Wisconsin 54942
USA

Tel: 920 757 1718
Website: www.minicrafttool.com

Glues and general crafts

Factory Direct Craft Supply
315 Conover Drive
Franklin
Ohio 45005
USA

Tel: (0800) 252 5223
Website: www.factorydirect.com

Wood supplies

Northeastern Scale Lumber Company
99 Cross Street
Mathuen
MA 01844
USA

Tel: 978 688 6019
Website: northeasternscalelumber.com

Terrific free graphics

Jim's Printable Minis
E-mail: jim@printmini.com
Website: www.printmini.com/gallery/

SWITZERLAND

Leather, foam sheeting and fabrics

Anna Lamour
(Angela Jones)
Bütenenhalde 62
6006 Luzern
Switzerland

At fairs internationally

About the Author

The textile arts have been a part of Janet Storey's life
for as long as she can remember. She had knitting
needles the same as her mother's and grandmother's
but half as long and was able to knit and crochet
before she went to school.

She was also taught embroidery and sewing at home.
For most of her life Janet took these skills for granted and
didn't consider them a career option; instead she trained
as a nurse but continued sewing and knitting in her spare
time, adding new skills all the time. It wasn't until poor
health ended her nursing career that she began to look
at her skills as a means of earning a living.

Janet's other passion is her dolls' house and she has
always tried to make as much as is feasibly possible
herself. This is partly for economic reasons but mostly
because she enjoys a challenge and learning new
skills. Janet admits that she uses her dolls' house as a
means of escaping into a fantasy world, where she
can lose herself for hours in a world entirely of her
own making. She thinks that dolls' houses are the
perfect hobby. No other hobby encompasses such
a huge range of skills and disciplines and the
possibilities are only limited by your imagination.

Index

GMC Publications
BOOKS

WOODCARVING

Beginning Woodcarving	*GMC Publications*
Carving Architectural Detail in Wood: The Classical Tradition	*Frederick Wilbur*
Carving Birds & Beasts	*GMC Publications*
Carving Classical Styles in Wood	*Frederick Wilbur*
Carving the Human Figure: Studies in Wood and Stone	*Dick Onians*
Carving Nature: Wildlife Studies in Wood	*Frank Fox-Wilson*
Celtic Carved Lovespoons: 30 Patterns	*Sharon Littley & Clive Griffin*
Decorative Woodcarving (New Edition)	*Jeremy Williams*
Elements of Woodcarving	*Chris Pye*
Figure Carving in Wood: Human and Animal Forms	*Sara Wilkinson*
Lettercarving in Wood: A Practical Course	*Chris Pye*
Relief Carving in Wood: A Practical Introduction	*Chris Pye*
Woodcarving for Beginners	*GMC Publications*
Woodcarving Made Easy	*Cynthia Rogers*
Woodcarving Tools, Materials & Equipment (New Edition in 2 vols.)	*Chris Pye*

WOODTURNING

Bowl Turning Techniques Masterclass	*Tony Boase*
Chris Child's Projects for Woodturners	*Chris Child*
Decorating Turned Wood: The Maker's Eye	*Liz & Michael O'Donnell*
Green Woodwork	*Mike Abbott*
A Guide to Work-Holding on the Lathe	*Fred Holder*
Keith Rowley's Woodturning Projects	*Keith Rowley*
Making Screw Threads in Wood	*Fred Holder*
Segmented Turning: A Complete Guide	*Ron Hampton*
Turned Boxes: 50 Designs	*Chris Stott*
Turning Green Wood	*Michael O'Donnell*
Turning Pens and Pencils	*Kip Christensen & Rex Burningham*
Wood for Woodturners	*Mark Baker*
Woodturning: Forms and Materials	*John Hunnex*
Woodturning: A Foundation Course (New Edition)	*Keith Rowley*
Woodturning: A Fresh Approach	*Robert Chapman*
Woodturning: An Individual Approach	*Dave Regester*
Woodturning: A Source Book of Shapes	*John Hunnex*
Woodturning Masterclass	*Tony Boase*
Woodturning Projects: A Workshop Guide to Shapes	*Mark Baker*

WOODWORKING

Beginning Picture Marquetry	*Lawrence Threadgold*
Carcass Furniture	*GMC Publications*
Celtic Carved Lovespoons: 30 Patterns	*Sharon Littley & Clive Griffin*
Celtic Woodcraft	*Glenda Bennett*
Celtic Woodworking Projects	*Glenda Bennett*
Complete Woodfinishing (Revised Edition)	*Ian Hosker*
David Charlesworth's Furniture-Making Techniques	*David Charlesworth*
David Charlesworth's Furniture-Making Techniques – Volume 2	*David Charlesworth*
Furniture Projects with the Router	*Kevin Ley*
Furniture Restoration (Practical Crafts)	*Kevin Jan Bonner*
Furniture Restoration: A Professional at Work	*John Lloyd*
Furniture Workshop	*Kevin Ley*
Green Woodwork	*Mike Abbott*
History of Furniture: Ancient to 1900	*Michael Huntley*
Intarsia: 30 Patterns for the Scrollsaw	*John Everett*
Making Heirloom Boxes	*Peter Lloyd*
Making Screw Threads in Wood	*Fred Holder*
Making Woodwork Aids and Devices	*Robert Wearing*
Mastering the Router	*Ron Fox*
Pine Furniture Projects for the Home	*Dave Mackenzie*
Router Magic: Jigs, Fixtures and Tricks to Unleash your Router's Full Potential	*Bill Hylton*
Router Projects for the Home	*GMC Publications*
Router Tips & Techniques	*Robert Wearing*
Routing: A Workshop Handbook	*Anthony Bailey*
Routing for Beginners (Revised and Expanded Edition)	*Anthony Bailey*
Stickmaking: A Complete Course	*Andrew Jones & Clive George*
Stickmaking Handbook	*Andrew Jones & Clive George*
Storage Projects for the Router	*GMC Publications*
Success with Sharpening	*Ralph Laughton*
Veneering: A Complete Course	*Ian Hosker*
Veneering Handbook	*Ian Hosker*
Wood: Identification & Use	*Terry Porter*
Woodworking Techniques and Projects	*Anthony Bailey*
Woodworking with the Router: Professional Router Techniques any Woodworker can Use	*Bill Hylton & Fred Matlack*

GARDENING

PHOTOGRAPHY

MAGAZINES

WOODTURNING ◆ WOODCARVING ◆ FURNITURE & CABINETMAKING
THE ROUTER ◆ NEW WOODWORKING ◆ THE DOLLS' HOUSE MAGAZINE
OUTDOOR PHOTOGRAPHY ◆ BLACK & WHITE PHOTOGRAPHY
KNITTING ◆ GUILD NEWS

The above represents a full list of all titles currently published or scheduled to be published.
All are available direct from the Publishers or through bookshops, newsagents and specialist retailers.
To place an order, or to obtain a complete catalogue, contact:

**GMC Publications,
166 High Street, Lewes, East Sussex BN7 1XU, United Kingdom
Tel: 01273 488005 Fax: 01273 402866
E-mail: pubs@thegmcgroup.com
www.gmcbooks.com**

Orders by credit card are accepted